GROWING
INTO
WHOLENESS

GROWING INTO WHOLENESS

Putting body, mind, and spirit back together

RANDY REESE, M.D.
FRANK MINIRTH, M.D.

MOODY PRESS
CHICAGO

134047

To those who hunger for wholeness.
It is our prayer that this book
will intensify their desire
and facilitate their quest for wholeness.

To our daughters,
Kathryn Leigh, Kristi Joy, and Ashley Anne (Dr. Reese);
Rachel, Renee, Carrie, and Alicia (Dr. Minirth).
It is our prayer that each embrace these principles
as her own and pass them on to future generations.

CONTENTS

ACKNOWLEDGMENTS

We are most grateful to our wives, Bonnie Ellen Reese and Mary Alice Minirth, whose sacrificial love and encouragement have helped to motivate us to complete this book. Their listening ears and insightful minds have contributed more than we will ever know, as God continues to make us of one heart. Each is our best friend, confidant, and advisor.

We express our deepest gratitude to Larry Weeden, whose editorial and writing expertise was absolutely essential to blend the experiences and minds of two physicians into a single manuscript. He has helped us fully express this vital message.

Special thanks to the staff at Moody Press. Duncan Jaenicke and Greg Thornton invested many hours listening to and reading our work; from the outset they have believed in the principles that we wanted to communicate and have guided us through the project of putting them into book form. They have kept us on track. We also give thanks to Jim Vincent, general editor, for putting the final editorial touches to the manuscript.

I (Randy) want to personally acknowledge those who, in God's sovereignty, have shaped the very person I am. My mother, Audrey Reese, always believed in me and encouraged me to pursue my dreams. During my high school and college years

George and Jane Baumgartner loved me like a son and became my spiritual parents by leading me to a saving knowledge of Jesus Christ.

Three individuals have shaped my professional and spiritual lives. Brad J. Cooper, M.D., a family physician and associate in private practice, was a challenging example to me during my first ten years of practicing medicine. I observed his confident, calm, and reassuring manner with his patients, his firm commitment to biblical medical ethics, and his uncompromising devotion to his family. His example has spoken much louder than any medical text or even a thousand sermons. Meanwhile, Skip and Buzzie Gray, active with the Navigators, have become adopted spiritual parents to Bonnie and myself, and spiritual grandparents to our daughters. Much of my worldview, my perspective on medicine as ministry, and my priorities on family have been gleaned from our intimate relationship with the Grays during the past twelve years.

Finally, I gratefully acknowledge my patients, many of whom you will meet in this book. They have been a source of encouragement and a challenge to excel as a physician. The personalities and life-messages of these individuals manifest themselves indirectly on the following pages. My special thanks to the surviving family of Clara Dawson, who have graciously allowed me to retell in chapter 10 her powerful story of faith.

INDEX OF CHARTS

Part 1

What Whole-Person Health Looks Like

1

SUZY'S NEW CHEVY MEETS THE TRAIN

Suzy Morgan, a working wife and mother of twin boys, had just finished a tough day at the office. *Finally, I can go home to Roger and the boys*, she thought as she hopped into the car. Driving home after a hard day's work, she began relaxing a little. Her pace, however, soon quickened.

About two miles from home, she approached the railroad tracks as she did every afternoon. But just before she started to cross over, her car died. The engine simply quit. Since she had slowed down to minimize the bumping of the railroad ties, the car coasted to a stop as soon as the front tires cleared the second rail. Her car was stalled right over the tracks. Instantly she felt irritation. *That's just great!* she thought. *What's wrong with the car now? This is the perfect ending to a perfect day!*

She tried to restart the car, but to no avail. *What's the problem here?* she wondered. *It ran fine on the way in this morning.* Then her eye caught the fuel gauge, and she realized she had run out of gas. *Oh, great! This is all I need now. Well, at least there's no train coming. Maybe if I hurry over to that station on the corner—*

At that moment, the railroad warning bells started to clang-clang, the gates descended, and a train whistle blew off to Suzy's left.

So far, inside Suzy, her physical senses had alerted her to several problems. First was the running out of gas; now a train was hurtling forward, perhaps unable to stop before hitting her car.

As this information passed from her eyes and ears into her mind in a fraction of a second, a part of her brain called the amygdala was stimulated, and it produced a fear response bordering on panic. Certain involuntary physical responses were triggered as a result: Adrenaline (also called epinephrine), a hormone secreted by the adrenal glands sitting atop the kidneys, pumped into the circulatory system, raising her heart rate and blood pressure. The blood vessels dilated to facilitate increased flow to the muscles, and her breathing rate accelerated as well so that she could either "fight or flee" better.

In the same instant, the information was passed to the cortex, another part of the brain, for analysis and decision making. In a flash she considered ideas like these: *Will the car start in time? Have I been able to restart the car before when I ran out of gas? How much time do I have? Will I have to get out of the car and run? Am I going to die?*

Only a fraction of a second had gone by, and she decided with her will to try again to start the car. As she turned the key, she was thinking, *This is a brand new car! We've only made three payments! If it's destroyed, the insurance will never cover the full cost of replacing it!*

The car just would not start, and a quick glance told her the train was fast approaching and probably wouldn't stop short of her position. In a full panic now, her body primed for action by her subconscious brain, she yanked on the door handle and shoved the door open, practically leapt out of the car, and sprinted the rest of the way across the tracks and well beyond the safety gate. Twenty seconds later, as the train was about to plow into her new Chevy, her muscles were still tensed for action, and she was ready to scream.

Watching her car get smashed to smithereens, she began to experience another emotional response. Its exact nature would depend on how attached she was to that car. If she wasn't too attached—if she saw the car as just a means of transportation and not as a precious possession—she might think and feel things like these: *Whew! What a relief! I got out just in time! Another half minute and it would have been curtains for me!*

Such a perspective might then lead naturally to a prayer like this: "Thank You, Lord, for sparing my life. Thank You that even though the car is gone, I got out unhurt. Thank You that the railroad signals worked, that the door didn't jam, that I didn't slip and fall as I tried to get away. Thank You that I'll still be able to grow old with my husband and watch my children grow up and some day hold my grandkids in my arms. Besides, everything we have belongs to You, including that car."

Suzy's spirit would have become involved in the incident at that point, if it hadn't been earlier. (She might have had the presence of mind to pray while she was still in the car.) And as she was praying like this, she might have noticed her heart and breathing starting to slow down toward normal, her nerves becoming less jittery, and her body temperature dropping just a little. The same mental and emotional processes that prepared her for the emergency would now be working in reverse, as the threat of imminent danger was recognized as being over.

On the other hand, if Suzy *was* very attached to the car, she might think and feel things like these: *You stupid car! Why did you have to pick a time like this to conk out on me! I could have been killed! This just isn't right! Wait a minute—it's Roger's fault! He used the car last night, and he was supposed to put some gas in it on his way home. Can't that man do anything right?*

That perspective might lead Suzy into a prayer like this: "God, why did You let this happen? I was almost killed! Is that what You want? Would You rob my little ones of their mother? Besides, You know the insurance won't cover the replacement cost of the car, so how am I supposed to get around? Don't You care about me anymore?"

Once again, Suzy's spirit would have become involved if it hadn't been already, only this time her physical excitation would not begin to return toward normal levels. Instead, this line of prayer would continue to feed the anxious and angry state of mind and the resulting physical readiness to "fight or flee" that was first created by the recognition of impending danger.

By now you may be feeling a lot of sympathy for Suzy, and you should have a fairly good idea of how the body, mind, and spirit—the three parts that make up the whole person—might interact in a real-life situation. They are interacting all the time; what's happening to us mentally affects us physically and spiritually as well. Even if our attention is focused on just one area, like the mental, all three parts are involved in everything we experience, all the time. That's why, if we want to pursue whole-person health, we have to understand that interaction.

But perhaps you can't identify too well with getting stuck on a set of railroad tracks as a train approaches. So let's consider a couple of other examples that illustrate the mind-body-spirit interplay.

You're sleeping soundly one night when the phone rings on the stand next to your bed. Fumbling for the handset, you look at the illuminated alarm clock and see it's 3:00 A.M. "Hello," you say groggily, wondering if you're about to be serenaded by a drunk.

But it's not a wino. It's your elderly mother, who lives across town, telling you she's got severe pain in her chest and has already called 911 for an ambulance.

Instantly, you're wide awake. Your heart is racing, and you've jumped to your feet, ready for action. Your mind is spinning: *Is it a heart attack? Will she even make it to the hospital? Which hospital will they take her to? How fast can I get there? Grandma died of a heart attack just two years ago!*

As you throw on some clothes and rush for the door, the name of the hospital on a scrap of paper in your hand, you send up a quick prayer that your dear mom will survive this terrible ordeal.

Or suppose your fifth-grade son brings home his weekly packet of schoolwork on Friday, and in the envelope is a sealed note from the teacher for you. Opening it, you read that she's concerned about your child's math performance. He seems to be struggling still with basic concepts in the current unit that the rest of the class is ready to move beyond.

Immediately, you feel a tightening in your stomach and the start of a tension headache. You've gone through this before, in every grade. *Why can't these teachers teach?!* you think. *My kid's not stupid!* But then an old fear comes back to haunt you: Maybe he is a little slower than most children. Maybe he'll never go to college or get a good job.

Next comes the hurt you've never outgrown since your own childhood: *He's just like me. He'll always be a little slower, and other people will pick on him all his life.*

Finally, you pray, "God, why couldn't You have spared him this? Why couldn't You give him a brighter future? Will he always have to feel inadequate like me?"

These three stories illustrate the interaction of the three parts that make up each of us. And as they show, the body, mind, and spirit are intimately connected. What happens in one part of us affects all the other parts. When there's a problem in one area, it's usually manifested in one or more of the others as well.

In fact, as doctors who often treat patients with psychological and spiritual as well as physical problems, we frequently see people whose very real physical symptoms originate not in the body but in the mind or spirit. We'll be telling a number of their stories (with certain details disguised to protect their privacy) in this book. And the point we want to make clearly is that, if we're going to enjoy complete and lasting health, we need to tend to all three parts of ourselves. Treating the physical symptoms alone will provide only temporary and superficial relief at best.

Our approach in this book is simple. We will consider first what authentic whole-person health looks like. Then we'll explore what usually goes wrong in our quest for such health, including the false promise of New Age thinking. Finally, we'll suggest how we can move from our current condition to the complete and lasting health we all desire.

Our beginning point, however, has to be a more thorough understanding of just how the three parts that make up each of us are interconnected—how what's going on in one affects the others as well. We turn our attention to the way those connections work in the next chapter.

TO YOUR HEALTH

1. If you had been in Suzy's place, what would have been your first thought as you heard the train approaching? Why? Would you have called on God for help?

2. How would you have responded emotionally to a call in the night saying your mother's health was failing? How might your emotions change over the next few hours?

3. What questions do you have for God about the way He created you? Your children (if you have any)?

    1. _____
    2. _____
    3. _____

4. When you're under extreme stress, what physical symptoms usually appear?

    1. _____
    2. _____
    3. _____

2

WHAT WE'RE MADE OF

Bart came into our clinic with several serious problems, all related, though neither he nor we knew it at first. What brought him to us was a physical disorder, an ulcer. He had a hole in the lining of his stomach, caused by the presence of excess acid. There has to be acid in the stomach, and the body produces it naturally, because that's how the food we eat gets broken down so it can be absorbed through the walls of the stomach and small intestine. But too much of anything, even good things, is usually a problem, and that's certainly the case with stomach acid.

What had caused Bart's ulcer? It seems he was worrying a lot—constantly, in fact—and he had been doing it for a long time. And worry, which is mental distress or preoccupation with a fear that something bad is going to happen, often stimulates the stomach to produce excess acid. So Bart's mental activity had led directly to a severe physical problem.

But that's not the end of the story. What was Bart worried about? The root of all his trouble was a spiritual issue. Bart was involved in an extramarital affair, and he was also a Christian. That means he knew what he was doing was wrong. Rather than deal with it in an appropriate spiritual way, however, he was living in rebellion against God's declaration against adultery, feeling guilty but continuing to behave immorally anyway.

No wonder he was worried so much. To flout God's clearly expressed will is a serious matter. In a person who has any conscience at all, such rebellion creates enormous guilt—spiritual pain. And when a person like Bart refuses to accept the spiritual remedy God offers, the result will be emotional pain as well, in the form of anxiety: *What will God do to me? What will happen to my marriage if my wife finds out? How much longer can I keep the affair hidden? What would my friends and fellow church members think? What effect would discovery have on my children?*

That's a lot to worry about, and, in Bart's case, it produced the excess flow of stomach acid that produced the ulcer he couldn't ignore. The physical problem forced him to seek help, but it was only the end result of a chain of spiritual and mental struggles.

We once had another patient, John, whose physical difficulty was also connected clearly to the rest of his being, but in reverse order. Like Bart, John had an ulcer. But in John's case, the cause was physical. His family had a history of ulcers, and in all probability there was an underlying genetic problem. He may have had only two layers in his stomach instead of the usual three, or perhaps his stomach produced more acid than normal.

In any event, the ulcer had deeply affected John mentally. He became consumed with worry. *What if the pain grows worse? What if the doctors can't find an effective treatment? What if I end up disabled and can no longer provide for my family?*

This kind of worry twisted John's emotions as well, making him irritable. He became difficult to get along with, overbearing toward his wife and children.

Finally, the illness also touched his spiritual life, causing him to doubt God's goodness and grace. "Why are You allowing this to happen to me?" he prayed. "What have I done to deserve this? It isn't fair!"

THE PARTS THAT MAKE UP THE WHOLE

Those two stories illustrate the truth that Scripture and human experience have indicated for millennia, namely, that human beings are made up of three distinct but interrelated parts. Paul referred to them all in 1 Thessalonians 5:23: "May God himself, the God of peace, sanctify you through and through. May your whole spirit, soul and body be kept blameless at the coming of our Lord Jesus Christ."

The three parts are also mentioned back at the creation of humanity in Genesis 2:7: "The Lord God formed man from the dust of the ground [the physical body] and breathed into his nostrils the breath of life [Hebrew word *neshamah,* meaning the human spirit], and man became a living being [Hebrew word *nephesh,* which can also be translated "soul"]."

Some philosophers and Bible scholars believe we're made up of only two parts: the outer, or material, part (the body) and the inner, or immaterial, part (consisting of the spirit and soul). Others, including ourselves, believe the elements of the inner person are distinct, and so we will discuss three separate parts of the individual—body, soul (or mind), and spirit.

Let's define each part briefly, and then we will consider how they are connected.

THE PHYSICAL BODY

The physical body we all possess is the outer man, the skin and bones and organs that together form systems (see Figure 1). Those systems have related functions and are vitally interdependent. Some, like the musculoskeletal (muscles and bones), are voluntary, meaning we control them by our choices. We decide whether to get up out of a chair, lift a box, pet a dog, or kick a soccer ball. The muscles that move the bones, and thus the whole body, contract and stretch in direct response to the exercise of our wills.

Other systems are involuntary, meaning we don't control them directly. Although we can regulate some of them a little with effort, for the most part they function on their own, without

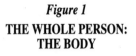

Figure 1
THE WHOLE PERSON:
THE BODY

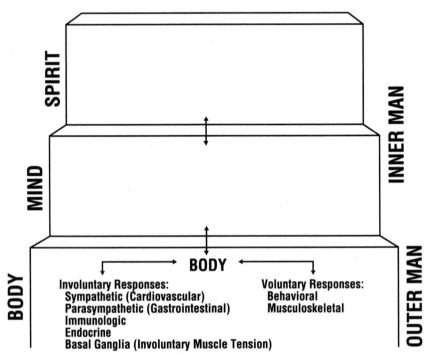

conscious thought. For example, the sympathetic nervous system controls the cardiovascular functions (the heart and blood vessels) that distribute life-giving blood. The parasympathetic nervous system controls the gastrointestinal functions (the stomach and intestines) with which we digest food and absorb it into the bloodstream. Among others we also have the immunologic system, which fights disease and infection, and the endocrine system, which includes organs like the pituitary gland that secrete substances to help control the body's functions.

The body's overall control center is the brain. The brain stem and cerebellum, two parts of the lower brain, direct such basic functions as breathing and muscular movement. Higher functions, such as memory, emotions, and thinking, take place in the limbic system and cerebral cortex; we'll say more about them shortly.

THE MIND

Next we have the inner man, which consists of the two remaining parts. The first of these is the mental, or psychological, dimension of a person, called the *psyche* in New Testament Greek. The mind, or soul, is that part of us that makes us each a unique individual (giving us our personality). The mind has three functions: intellect, emotions, and volition, or will (see Figure 2). It also monitors the autonomic nervous system, which controls such vital functions as breathing. (We are unaware of most of these functions.) Sometimes referred to as the soul for the unique elements it imparts to each individual, our mind lets us comprehend and analyze data from our environment as perceived by the five senses.

We also understand complex and abstract ideas, which gives us tremendous potential for creativity. That's surely part of what it means to be made in God's image. And this capacity for abstract thinking, coupled with the human spirit, also gives us the ability to comprehend the unseen spiritual realities of life.

This creative and spiritual aspect is what sets us apart mentally from all other life on earth. In addition, we can reflect

Figure 2
THE WHOLE PERSON:
THE MIND

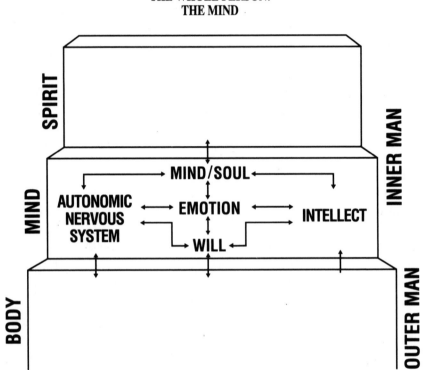

on the remote past with our memory and also anticipate the distant future, which gives us the unique ability to worship God by praising Him for past faithfulness and trusting Him for future provision.

In our minds, each of us has a belief system that greatly influences our emotions and will and, ultimately, our speech and behavior. This is the core of what we hold to be true about ourselves and the world around us. Our beliefs are shaped first by our parents and later by teachers, peers, television, church, and a host of other influences.

We refine our beliefs as we mature and begin to think for ourselves, yet early influences can be powerful and hard to change. We've seen many women, unfortunately, who were abused as children and then told they were no good by their parents as a way of justifying the abuse. This often leads to "toxic shame," a depressive emotion unlike genuine, realistic shame that results from violating God's revealed will. Having that poor self-image ingrained in them, the women continue as adults to interpret the world around them in a way that reinforces their belief. They often marry abusive men, for example, feeling mistreatment is just what they deserve.

That raises the point that each of us perceives reality differently depending on our training and experience, and that all behavior—even irrational behavior—has a purpose when seen from the individual's point of view. A person who is generally healthy but depressed will likely interpret reality pessimistically and act accordingly. Another person with a biochemical imbalance in the brain may become psychotic and lose touch with the reality the rest of us know, yet that person's distorted world seems as real as real can be to him or her.

Because the mind directs how we think, feel, and act, it's not surprising that Satan works hard to make us all believe his lies about God, the world, and ourselves. Satan also encourages us to deal with the shame (loss of self-esteem) and guilt (fear of abandonment by God) we feel when we think we've done wrong by using one or more defense mechanisms. (More about them in chapter 5.) We need the truth of God's revealed

Word to serve as the objective lens through which we interpret reality. And that is why, after urging us to present our bodies to Christ as a living sacrifice, Paul immediately added, "Do not conform any longer to the pattern of this world, but be transformed by the renewing of your mind" (Romans 12:2). We'll say more about this in chapter 8, where we discuss the process of moving from sickness to health.

The second function of our minds is to experience emotions. Pleasurable emotions help us to enjoy intimacy with God and others, whereas painful emotions serve to warn us about unresolved psychological or spiritual problems in the same way that physical pain warns us about an underlying injury or illness.

The part of the brain that processes emotions is called the limbic system. It consists of several centers where nerve cells are connected by nerve bundles to form a circuit. When we're experiencing an emotion, electrical activity is going around and around in this circuit. And when it's a negative emotion such as fear or unresolved anger, that activity will continue, either consciously or unconsciously and for years if necessary, until the conflict that created it is resolved.

Suppose, for instance, that a child was injured in an extremely frightening way—perhaps her family had a serious automobile accident at night, with a lot of noise and glaring lights and strange people crowding around, and she became separated from her parents for a while. A young child's mind may be unable to handle that kind of experience, to analyze just what happened and why, but it will remember the fear.

To keep from being paralyzed with fear, the child's mind may unconsciously repress the negative emotion—stuff it, try to forget it. And that may work in terms of keeping the fear out of the child's conscious mind. But the negative emotion is still there, going around and around in the limbic system.

As an adult, this individual will continue to experience more fear and anxiety than the average person and won't even know why. And when confronted with a situation that naturally produces a little bit of fear—perhaps driving on a rain-slickened road at night—that subconscious fear from the past will augment the fear of the moment and create an unusually intense anxiety that's out of proportion to the circumstances. Both that person and others will be surprised when he or she "overreacts" to the situation at hand.

A key part of the limbic system is the thalamus, an early processing station that receives input from the five senses and passes it on to the cortex for analysis. However, if a situation is perceived as threatening, information may be passed directly from the thalamus to the amygdala, a tiny, almond-shaped structure that some scientists call "emotion central." It makes a quick assessment of what's happening and may produce a primitive reaction of fear or anxiety, then send that message on to the cortex for further thinking and enhancement through memory. It may also set in motion such basic involuntary bodily responses as quickened heart rate and breathing, increased blood pressure, and sweating. In essence, we may feel before we think.

The third function of our minds is to make choices of thought, word, and action. This is the human will.

Our wills are driven to varying extents by our motives, and the intensity of a motive will determine the intensity of our emotions when our will has been thwarted. A man whose life's goal was to become a concert pianist, for example, may well become angry or depressed if he ends up as a high school music teacher instead. However, someone whose goal was simply to please God by being the best piano player he could be might have an easier time trusting God and finding contentment as a music teacher.

Our wills often determine our beliefs. As an old saying goes, "When you have a hammer in your hand, everything looks like a nail." We tend to see and believe what we want to see (or at least expect to see) and believe. We've all encountered the pushy parent who is absolutely convinced her child is going to be a great actor or baseball player or whatever, so every halfway good thing the child does is perceived as a mark of brilliance. More objective observers might say the child has average ability, but that parent is certain her child is a budding superstar, and nothing will convince her otherwise.

Ultimately, our will determines how we behave. We say and do what we choose to say and do. God made us to be responsible beings.

THE SPIRIT

The human spirit (*pneuma* in New Testament Greek) is the second part of the inner man, and it, like the soul (or mind, which we will use as an interchangeable term), is eternal. Unlike the physical body, which from the point of birth to death is undergoing a process of decay, the inner man will live forever (see 2 Corinthians 4:16-18).

In some ways, it's difficult to distinguish the soul from the spirit. How do we really separate them? *Vine's Expository Dictionary of New Testament Words* puts it this way: "The language of Heb. 4:12 suggests the extreme difficulty of distinguishing between the soul and the spirit, alike in their nature and in their activities. Generally speaking the spirit is the higher, the soul the lower element. The spirit may be recognized as the life principle bestowed on man by God, the soul as the resulting life constituted in the individual, the body being the material organism animated by soul and spirit."[1]

From a functional point of view, our spiritual dimension consists of the human spirit and conscience (see Figure 3). Those who have received the Lord Jesus Christ as their spiritual Savior also have the Holy Spirit residing in this part of them: "Don't you know that you yourselves are God's temple and that God's Spirit lives in you?" (1 Corinthians 3:16). Let's consider each of these parts.

The human spirit is our "spiritual sense organ." It gives us all a God-consciousness, which in non-Christians is distorted: on their own, they are unable to understand the true God, although they do know He exists (Romans 1:19-21). All people everywhere have had gods, but in most cases they have been the false gods the human mind invents when it rejects the truth about the one God of the universe (see Romans 1:18-32). When regenerated by the Holy Spirit, however, the human spirit has

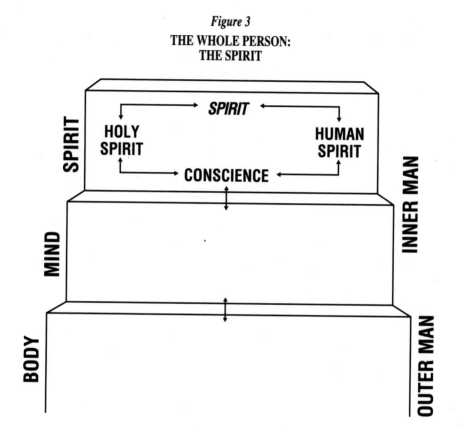

Figure 3
THE WHOLE PERSON:
THE SPIRIT

the ability to perceive, understand (to a limited degree), and fellowship with God.

The conscience is our God-given, inborn faculty that tells right from wrong. It prompts us to think wholesome thoughts and to speak and act in a morally upright way. It condemns unwholesome thoughts and immoral behavior. We don't need to be taught, for example, that robbery and murder are wrong; we simply know these things to be true.

The conscience can be shaped by parents and the influences of society, however, so that it goes toward either of two extremes. On the one hand, in today's lax and amoral society, it's not unusual for individuals to have a seared and insensitive conscience to the point that right has become wrong and wrong has become right. Morals have become relative to their "needs" and the situation at hand. Extramarital sex, for example, which God's Word and a clear conscience condemn, is now considered OK between any two consenting adults as long as "no one is hurt."

On the other hand, people raised in a rigid, legalistic, punitive environment can develop a hypersensitive conscience that condemns any deviation from their standards. They may also experience false guilt when they think or do something that violates those standards but in no way violates a biblical command or principle.

When we become Christians and are regenerated by the Holy Spirit, however, our consciences are also regenerated and sensitized to God's moral will for our lives. As God said, "I will put my laws in their minds and write them on their hearts. I will be their God, and they will be my people" (Hebrews 8:10).

The conscience can be viewed as the moral link between spirit and soul (see Figure 3). When our conscience is clear and we live according to it, we have peace of mind. When it is violated, we feel guilt and shame, which are spiritual emotions arising out of our inherent knowledge of God, the Law-giver. Guilt is an anxious emotion in which we fear abandonment (loss of relationship) by the Law-giver. Shame is a depressive emotion in which we experience or grieve the loss of self-esteem because of our failure to live up to the expectations of the Law-maker. Those feelings, if left unresolved, can result in physical disease, as we saw in Bart's chapter-opening story.

The Holy Spirit is, of course, the third Person of the Trinity. This is not a theological text, so we won't dwell on the subject, but one point needs to be made that's relevant to what we're talking about here.

The clear lesson of both Scripture and experience is that we are incapable of living emotionally and spiritually healthy lives on our own. Because of our sin nature, we will make wrong choices and violate our consciences if all we have to draw on is our own strength. Only the power of the indwelling Holy Spirit makes it possible to live in a way that pleases God. As He Himself said, " 'Not by [human] might nor by power, but by my Spirit,' says the Lord Almighty" (Zechariah 4:6).

So the active presence of the Spirit is essential to whole-person health. We like the way authors Gary Smalley and John Trent put it in their book *The Two Sides of Love*: "Depending on our own power . . . is like trying to push a car down the street instead of using its engine. We may be able to go a short distance, but each step further drains our energy and invites frustration. Is there a better way? The truth is, there's only one way, one source of power to truly change our lives for good and maintain those changes for a lifetime."[2]

We'll be describing a number of ways to experience better health in this book, but always remember that when it comes to making the right choices and acting on them, we need the empowering of the Holy Spirit. For a fuller discussion of what it means to live in submission to the Lord in the power of the Spirit, see the booklet *My Heart Christ's Home*, by Robert Boyd Munger.

THE HIP BONE'S CONNECTED TO THE THIGH BONE—AND A LOT MORE

Now that we've reviewed the parts that make up the whole person, let's look at a specific incident to see more of how they're connected and work together. Remember Suzy

Morgan, whose encounter with the train began chapter 1? Let's go back to the beginning of that day in the Morgan household and see what happened with her. Before the grand finale on the railroad tracks, Suzy's day was becoming one galloping mess.

Suzy and Roger and the twins, Billy and Brad, normally have little trouble getting ready for the day. But this Monday morning in the Morgan home got off to a rough start, especially for Suzy. Her day started when the neighbor's dog began barking loudly at 4:30 A.M. Seems he needed to be let out to answer nature's call. Suzy, a light sleeper, was unable to get back to sleep and so greeted the dawn baggy-eyed while hugging a cup of coffee. (Spot was contentedly snoring again by then.)

Shortly after she woke the twins, Suzy had to start playing referee. She settled who got to use the toilet first. Then she decided who would get the last of the Fritos® for lunch, which left Billy pouting.

As she raced off to finish getting herself ready for work, aware she was at least five minutes behind schedule, Suzy heard Roger call from the bedroom, "Honey, this button just came off my shirt. Can you put it back on? I've got a big meeting today, and you know this shirt is my favorite."

"Sure," she said with a hint of resignation that Roger totally missed. As she reached into her sewing chest to find a needle and thread, she couldn't help thinking, *Will he ever learn to sew his own buttons back on?* Realizing he probably never would, she grabbed the shirt from him, sat on the edge of the bed, and began sewing as fast as she could.

Just as Suzy finished with the shirt, Brad ran into the room shouting, "Mommy, Daddy, something's burning in the kitchen!"

The eggs! Suzy thought. Dashing to the kitchen, she saw that breakfast now resembled a collection of hockey pucks in a pan. She opened a window to air out the room, but not in time—the smoke alarm blasted her ears and made her jump. When her heart started beating again a few seconds later, she set the pan aside and reached for another. *No time to clean that one now; I'll just do some more eggs quickly.*

Opening the refrigerator and taking out the egg carton,

she saw she had just enough left for three people. *Well, maybe I can run by McDonald's after I drop the kids off*, she figured.

Twenty minutes later, Suzy had to break up a toothpaste war between the twins. (Roger had already left for his work.) *Why isn't Roger ever here at times like this?* she thought. She was dimly aware that a headache was growing at the back of her head. As she pushed the kids out to the garage and climbed into her car, she noticed a run in the side of the right leg of her pantyhose. *No time to go back and change now,* she thought as she reminded the twins to buckle up.

Driving to the day-care center, Suzy let out a sigh of relief. At last they were on their way, even if it was twenty minutes late. *Mr. Taylor will understand,* she told herself. *After all, it's Monday morning. But I'll need to take some aspirin when I get there.*

A few minutes later, Suzy pulled into the day-care center's parking lot. As she held the door open for the twins, a familiar stab of guilt pierced her heart. *Stop it!* she admonished herself. *They're doing fine here.* Shaking off the feeling, she waved good-bye and drove away. The churning in her stomach, she realized, was only partly the result of hunger.

Approaching McDonald's, Suzy glanced at her watch. *No time to stop after all*, she realized with a sigh. *Maybe I can grab one of those sweet rolls from the vending machine on my way upstairs. So much for the diet.*

Because she was late arriving, she had to park in the far corner of the office lot. Half walking, half running, sweat dampening her forehead, she hurried to her desk as fast as she could, only glancing at the vending machine as she sped by. A quick look at the wall clock as she dropped her purse on her desk told her it was now twenty-five minutes past her starting time. *Well, at least I got in without being noticed*, she told herself, pulling open the drawer where she kept her aspirin. *On an empty stomach?* she asked as she looked at the bottle. Her head was now pounding, however, so she went ahead and took a couple.

There have been too many Monday mornings like this recently, she realized as she tried to calm down and cool off.

It's become normal for a million things to go wrong and for me to be way late. Her growing awareness of a small but sharp pain in the area of her stomach made her think, *Good grief! Am I getting an ulcer now? I'm too young for ulcers!*

"Good morning, Suzy! So nice you could join us today! Did we have a little trouble on the way in?"

Mr. Taylor's sarcastic voice, coming from behind her, caught Suzy by surprise and made her heart leap and her head pound all the more.

"Good morning, Mr. Taylor," she said nervously as she turned to face him. "I did have a few problems. The kids were fighting from the time they got up, I had an accident fixing breakfast—"

"Spare me the details!" he said, interrupting. "I suppose I should be used to this by now." That nasty remark brought a fresh stab of pain in Suzy's stomach and more sweat to her forehead. "Dear God —" she started to pray before stopping abruptly. *It's been a long time since I really prayed*, she suddenly realized. *I guess I haven't felt like it much, especially on Monday mornings. Come to think of it, I haven't been reading my Bible, either. God seems so far away these days.*

Maybe you've had a day as bad as Suzy's started out to be. We could all tell stories of days we'll never forget—no matter how hard we try! But besides illustrating Murphy's Law run amok (anything that can go wrong, will), her story also shows the intimate connection between the human body, mind, and spirit. The three parts are so closely tied together, in fact, that illnesses showing up in one part of a person often have their real origin in another part. As doctors, then, when a patient comes to us with a particular problem, like Bart with his ulcer at the beginning of this chapter, we have at least two jobs to do. First, we have to treat the immediate illness. But second, we also have to look for any underlying problem that might be the root cause of the sickness.

The following is just a partial list of illnesses that may show up in one part of a person even though they originated in another:

1. *Psychological problems with physical causes.* Excessive *anxiety* can grow out of many physical conditions, such as tumors, mitral valve prolapse (a heart ailment underlying 30 to 40 percent of feelings of panic), hormone abnormalities, and hyperthyroidism. *Depression* can be caused by hepatitis, pneumonia, stroke, multiple sclerosis (MS), rheumatoid arthritis, drugs, and alcohol, among other things. *Personality changes* can develop from viral illnesses, epilepsy, MS, and senility. *Amnesia* may stem from seizure disorder, stroke, trauma (typically a blow to the head), and alcohol abuse.

2. *Spiritual problems with physical causes.* With abnormal religious preoccupation, a person becomes obsessed with religious issues, such as a continuing sense of guilt about his actions or a harsh, fault-finding attitude toward others. Such an obsession can result from epilepsy, manic-depressive psychosis, obsessive-compulsive disorder, and drugs.

3. *Physical problems with emotional causes.* Stress can lower resistance to infection and lead to illnesses or diseases, such as colds, pneumonia, and cancer. Loneliness may contribute to coronary artery disease and cancer. So great is the grief after the death of a spouse that widows often succumb to death themselves in the first year after their mate dies.

4. *Spiritual problems with psychological causes.* Obsessive-compulsive disorder (OCD) may lead people to think they're not saved or have committed the unpardonable sin. Not everyone who questions his or her spiritual condition has a psychological problem, of course. But OCD can have the effect mentioned on good Christian people. The cause may be biochemical; OCD may originate from an imbalance of serotonin metabolism and is effectively treated with medications that restore the normal levels of serotonin. Psychotic disorders frequently cause patients to exhibit false religious preoccupation.

5. Physical problems with spiritual causes. Bart's ulcer, described in the opening of this chapter, was caused by his tremendous sense of guilt in having an affair when he knew God calls adultery sin. Guilt or spiritual legalism can lead to physical ailments.

6. Psychological problems with spiritual causes. At times people may respond to the stress of ignoring or rejecting spiritual values with psychological problems. When people let temporal values (for instance, seeking wealth or wanting a new car) rule their lives instead of operating with eternal values, anxiety or depression may result.

We could continue to list ailments that show up in one part of a person even though they originate in another, but you get the picture. And again, for the problems we did name, our list of causes was only partial. A problem in one area clearly influences the entire individual.

Now we have seen what we're made of and how the three parts of a person are intimately connected. Our illustrations have been of people who had problems in all three areas. But when all the parts of a person are working together in a proper way, what does that look like? What's the picture of whole-person health we should all be trying to achieve? We'll explore that next, then give you a chance to evaluate your own health with a simple self-test.

To Your Health

1. Think of someone you know who had a problem in one area that actually originated in another. What happened?

2. In which part of your person do you seem to have had the most difficulties? Why do you think that is?

3. What are some of the core ideas about yourself in your belief system? About others? About God?

4. How do you respond to a person who has a lax conscience? Why? To a person with a hypersensitive conscience? Why?

3

THE PICTURE OF HEALTH

A beautiful young lady named Shirley came to our clinic one time in tremendous pain. Tests revealed she had a chronic connective tissue disease called sarcoidosis. Such a disease can attack any organ of the body and cause significant pain, and in Shirley's case the pain was especially acute in the joints.

Whenever someone endures that kind of continual physical pain, there's going to be emotional suffering as well. It's wearing and hope-sapping. And Shirley, though she was a wonderfully mature Christian, was no exception. She had the same concerns and questions that anyone would in her situation.

She chose to deal with her suffering in a healthy manner, however. She didn't bottle up the physical and emotional pain and spiritual questions but instead discussed them openly with us and others. And rather than surround herself with people who would shower her with pity, she chose to have healthy people around her, people who affirmed her faith in God and helped her focus on the good in her life. In other words, she developed a genuine support system that enabled her to make the most of her life rather than *dis*abling her.

Simply put, Shirley chose the healthy way to deal with her pain in all its forms. Shirley's story illustrates several crucial truths about whole-person health that we'll be developing in this chapter. Perhaps the most important of these is that, while pain is inevitable, misery is optional. Notice that we said Shirley *chose* the healthy way to handle her pain, and that's a power we all possess. Difficulties of one kind or another come into every life; how we respond to them, and how we view life generally, determines our quality of life.

MENTAL AND EMOTIONAL HEALTH

People who are mentally and emotionally healthy maintain a positive mental attitude. They don't deny life's hard side, but they also don't forget that there's a lot of good and beauty in the world. They see each new day as a fresh opportunity to learn, to grow, and to love. They know they're loved by God and others, and they believe that their loving God ultimately works all things together for good, so they have hope in the core of their being (see Jeremiah 29:11; Romans 8:28).

In keeping with that attitude, healthy people laugh frequently and easily. They don't waste a lot of time worrying or getting cynical about the faults of others. And they don't let bitterness take root in their souls. They're interested in other people, and they develop solid friendships. They're comfortable with who and what they are and feel free to be themselves in front of others.

How can a person respond that way when pain is so common to our lives? We'll say more about how that kind of health is developed in chapter 8. But for now, let's consider those criteria in the case of Shirley. Did she have a positive mental attitude? She couldn't deny the reality of her illness, yet she did keep a positive outlook on life. She continued to enjoy the good in her experience. She stayed close to her friends and let them encourage her. She never lost her sense of humor but remained a fun person to be around, even as she talked candidly about her condition. Naturally, she was concerned about the future course of her disease, but she wasn't consumed by worry, nor did she grow bitter toward God or anyone else.

Maintaining such a level of mental and emotional health isn't easy, and it's certainly not automatic, even for Christians, though they have an invaluable foundation of faith from which to face life's storms (see Luke 6:46-49).

Now, these aspects of mental and emotional health may not sound all that dramatic or outstanding. But in working with the many people who come to us for help, we know how difficult it is to maintain such health and how easily people develop unhealthy ways of dealing with life.

Think about it for a minute: How many people do you know who have what you would call a positive, healthy, yet realistic mental attitude—people who are enjoyable to be around and who feed your own sense of hope? In contrast, how many people do you know who are basically negative in their outlook, who complain in ways subtle or obvious, worry, are dissatisfied with their lot in life, or often seem bitter? If your experience is anything like ours, you know a good many more of the latter than of the former.

That's why real mental and emotional health is a significant accomplishment. It doesn't come naturally, and if it were easy, everyone would have it.

SPIRITUAL HEALTH

The picture of spiritual health can be drawn with parallels to the basics of physical health. When you boil down the essentials for keeping the body humming along, you're left with four things: eating nutritious foods, breathing clean air, getting adequate rest, and exercising regularly. Let's look at how spiritual health compares.

We definitely need good nourishment if we're to grow and thrive spiritually. In this case, our essential "food" is God's Word, the Bible. The healthy person partakes of it regularly in reading, study, meditation, and application. If we were to write a prescription for spiritual fitness, it would include a large daily dose of scriptural input.

A strong example to us comes from the Bible itself, in the person of an easily overlooked hero of the Old Testament. His name was Ezra, and "he was a teacher well versed in the Law of Moses" (Ezra 7:6). About thirteen years before Nehemiah went to Jerusalem to rebuild the city walls, Ezra received a commission from the Persian King Artaxerxes to go to Jerusalem and appoint magistrates and judges for the entire region. While he was there, Ezra led the Jews in what we today would call a revival.

Why was he such an effective leader? The Bible tells us, "The gracious hand of his God was on him. For Ezra had devoted himself to the study and observance of the Law of the Lord, and to teaching its decrees and laws in Israel" (Ezra 7:9-10).

The healthy, spiritual breathing each person needs is prayer, conversing with the Lord. That means expressing to Him our attitudes and feelings, as well as listening to His still, small voice. And just as we need to breathe air steadily—we can't stop for long without dying—so we're to "pray without ceasing" (1 Thessalonians 5:17, KJV*). That doesn't mean spending all our time on our knees or with our eyes closed, but keeping our hearts and minds tuned to Him constantly, talking to Him as a friend and Lord who is always with us.

Christian fellowship is the spiritual parallel to physical rest. Fellowship occurs when we gather together to worship, to learn from each other and the Word, and to help bear each other's burdens. When true fellowship exists, it offers a level of understanding and support that can't be found anywhere else in human experience. And when we leave a gathering in which we've been a part of such fellowship, we are greatly refreshed and ready to face life's challenges and opportunities once again.

Finally, the parallel to physical exercise is witnessing, telling others the good news of the gospel. That communication can take many forms, but they all involve putting forth effort to let others know about the peace of God that is ours through faith in Christ. When we do that, we are offering others peace with God as well.

*King James Version

The kind of loving, supportive fellowship we just described can also be one of the most powerful forms of witness. That was certainly the case in the early days of the church. "They devoted themselves to the apostles' teaching and to the fellowship, to the breaking of bread and to prayer. Every day they continued to meet together in the temple courts. They broke bread in their homes with glad and sincere hearts, praising God and enjoying the favor of all the people. And the Lord added to their number daily those who were being saved" (Acts 2:42, 46-47).

When we witness, we have to overcome our natural fears, and we often find ourselves questioned and challenged. This is good exercise for our spiritual muscles. Nothing helps us understand our own faith better than having to explain and defend it to a non-Christian.

PHYSICAL HEALTH

We come now to physical health, and we've saved it until last for a couple of reasons. One is that it has already been the subject of numerous articles, books, and TV and radio shows, so you may already know a good deal about it. But the other is that in many ways, it's the health area of least importance. As Shirley demonstrated, you can be very sick physically, yet if you're strong emotionally and spiritually, you can still have a satisfying, worthwhile life. On the other hand, you can be a tower of physical strength, but if you're not right emotionally or spiritually, you can be extremely miserable.

Our culture, sadly, seems to have these facts reversed. Physical fitness, youthful appearance, and sexual desirability are extolled endlessly, and billions of dollars are spent annually in pursuit of them. The message given out and believed by all too many is that if you look young, feel great, and turn heads, you've "got it made." A life of nonstop excitement is yours for the taking.

The truth, of course, is that good physical health doesn't mean looking like a twenty-year-old forever. It means having the energy and vitality to work, to meet the needs of your family (including a monogamous sexual relationship with your spouse), to enjoy God's creation, and to serve Him.

In the previous section, we mentioned the four broad elements of physical health. Now we'll get specific about good physical habits, and in chapters 8 and 9 we will say even more about how we can change to and maintain such habits.

The key to good nutrition is to eat a balanced diet. This alone could reduce annual cancer deaths by one-third. A variety of foods in each of the four food groups should be consumed daily: fruits, vegetables, meats and dairy products, and grains. Healthy people eat plenty of high-fiber foods and limit their intake of fat. They also limit their consumption of smoked, salt-cured, and nitrite-preserved foods, of salt, and of refined sugar. They make sure they get enough calcium, and they avoid fad diets.

Breathing well is closely related to aerobic exercise, which strengthens the heart and enlarges lung capacity. This means vigorous exercise for at least twenty minutes at a time, at least three times a week.

Exercise may well be the single most important thing we can do to extend our lives. It gives us more energy, helps to control weight, reduces cholesterol, and generally makes us feel better by releasing chemicals within the body called endorphins.

Physically healthy people also keep their weight within five to ten pounds of the ideal for their sex and height. They know that obesity (being more than 10 percent over the ideal) increases the risk of death from heart disease and cancer. One study concluded that for every pound of excess weight gained after age thirty, a person's life span is shortened by six months.[1] (By the way, 38 percent of American females and 31 percent of the males are overweight.)

Cholesterol control is also important, as high levels have been proved to be associated with coronary artery disease and heart attack. For every 1 percent reduction in total cholesterol, the risk of heart attack is lowered by 2 percent.[2]

Adequate rest usually means six to eight hours of sleep per night, or even as much as ten depending on individual physiology. Our minds and bodies urgently need that relaxation and renewing. Generally, however, our sleep requirements decrease with age, from the eighteen to twenty hours per day of newborns to less than six hours per day for some adults, especially senior citizens.

Here are a few other guidelines that contribute to good physical health:

- Never use tobacco in any form. It contributes to all four of the top killers in the United States—heart attack, stroke, cancer, and emphysema.
- Use alcohol moderately or not at all. It's associated with hypertension, various cancers, and cirrhosis of the liver, as well as more than half of our highway fatalities.
- Avoid exposure to dangerous substances like radon, asbestos, pesticides, and toxic wastes.
- Avoid too much sun, and use protective covering or sun screen when exposed. Chronic exposure accelerates the aging of skin and increases the risk of skin cancer.

HOW HEALTHY ARE YOU?

Now that we've painted briefly a picture of whole-person health, we'd like to give you an opportunity to measure, informally, just how healthy you are in all the parts of your person. In the self-test that follows, you'll find twenty-nine partial statements, each followed by several different possible ways to complete it. For each statement, check the ending that most closely matches your current lifestyle. Be objective and honest in your answers; no one else has to see which ones you've checked.

Each answer is followed by a point value in parentheses. At the end of each section, total your point values to get an idea of how healthy you are in that area of your life. (Notice that for the purpose of this quiz, we've added a separate section on social health.) And at the end of the instrument, record your totals from every section to get an overall picture of your health. If you're like us, you will feel good about where you stand in some areas and see a need for improvement in at least one other.

YOUR HEALTH PROFILE

PHYSICAL HEALTH

1. I am:
    ___ More than 50 pounds overweight (1)
    ___ 26-50 pounds overweight (2)
    ___ 11-25 pounds overweight (3)
    ___ Within 10 pounds of my ideal weight (4)

2. I exercise hard (more than 20 minutes at a time):
    ___ Not at all (1)
    ___ 1-2 times per week (2)
    ___ 3-4 times per week (3)
    ___ More than 4 times weekly (4)

3. My diet consists of:
    ___ Mostly fast foods (1)
    ___ Eating out at least half the time (2)
    ___ Meat and potatoes (3)
    ___ Mostly well-planned meals, with a variety of fruits, vegetables, fiber, fish, and poultry, and limited amounts of fatty or fried foods and red meats (4)

4. My cholesterol level is:
    ___ Higher than normal (1)
    ___ Normal (check this if not known) (2)
    ___ Below normal (3)

5. I sleep restfully:
    ___ Less than 6 hours per night (1)
    ___ 6-8 hours per night (2)
    ___ 8-10 hours per night (3)

6. I use alcohol:
   ___ Regularly, often exceeding two drinks daily (1)
   ___ Regularly, but no more than two drinks daily (2)
   ___ On occasion (3)
   ___ Rarely (4)
   ___ Not at all (5)

7. I smoke:
   ___ Regularly, more than 2 packs daily (1)
   ___ Regularly, between 1 and 2 packs per day (2)
   ___ Regularly, but less than 1 pack per day (3)
   ___ Rarely or on occasion (4)
   ___ Never (5)

8. My blood pressure is:
   ___ Higher than normal (1)
   ___ Normal (to the best of my knowledge) (2)
   ___ Lower than normal (3)

   Physical Health Score: ___
24-31	Good
16-23	Fair
Less than 16	Poor

MENTAL AND EMOTIONAL HEALTH

9. I love to read:
   ___ Never (1)
   ___ On occasion (2)
   ___ Regularly (3)

10. I engage in hobbies:
    ___ Never (1)
    ___ Occasionally (2)
    ___ Regularly (3)

11. When I think about myself, my thoughts are usually:
    ___ Negative (1)
    ___ Both negative and positive (2)
    ___ Positive (3)

12. When I spend time with friends, we laugh:
   ___ Never (1)
   ___ Rarely (2)
   ___ Occasionally (3)
   ___ Frequently (4)

13. I tend to worry:
   ___ All the time (1)
   ___ Frequently (2)
   ___ Rarely or occasionally (3)
   ___ Never (4)

14. It's easy for me to hold a grudge:
   ___ Whenever anyone offends me (1)
   ___ When I'm hurt deeply by another (2)
   ___ Hardly ever (3)

15. I usually handle conflict by:
   ___ Avoiding it (1)
   ___ Avoiding it for a time, but eventually working things out (2)
   ___ Promptly attempting to work out a solution (3)

16. I tend to be cynical:
   ___ Most of the time (1)
   ___ On occasion (2)
   ___ Rarely or not at all (3)

17. I tend to get angry:
   ___ At the slightest mistake or offense (1)
   ___ Over major mistakes or offenses (2)
   ___ Rarely (3)

18. I feel sad, blue, or depressed:
   ___ Most of the time (1)
   ___ Occasionally for no reason (2)
   ___ Rarely (3)
   ___ Usually only following a major loss (4)

Mental and Emotional Health Score: ___

24-33	Good
14-23	Fair
Less than 14	Poor

SOCIAL HEALTH

19. I have:
  ___ No friends at all whom I could call upon in an emer-
      gency (1)
  ___ A few friends, but none I can share my true feelings
      with (2)
  ___ Many friends, but none I can share my true feelings
      with (3)
  ___ Many friends, including one or two I can share my
      true feelings with (4)

20. When interacting with others, I tend to:
  ___ Put on a facade with most (1)
  ___ "Be real" with close friends, but put on a facade with
      others (2)
  ___ "Be real" with most people (3)

21. Sexually I have had:
  ___ Multiple homosexual partners (1)
  ___ Multiple heterosexual partners (2)
  ___ A few heterosexual partners (3)
  ___ Two heterosexual partners (4)
  ___ One heterosexual partner (5)

22. I invest meaningful interactive time with family members:
  ___ Rarely (less than 2 hours/week) (1)
  ___ Occasionally (2-4 hours/week) (2)
  ___ Relatively consistently (5-8 hours/week) (3)
  ___ Consistently (9 or more hours/week) (4)

  Social Health Score: _____
    13-16   Good
    9-12   Fair
    Less than 9 Poor

SPIRITUAL HEALTH

23. I would describe my relationship with God as:
    ___ Nonexistent (1)
    ___ Distant (2)
    ___ Superficial (I go to church and do religious things, but I don't feel close to Him.) (3)
    ___ Growing gradually closer to Him (4)
    ___ Intimately personal, and deepening every day (5)

24. I spend meaningful, personal time in God's Word and prayer:
    ___ Rarely or not at all (1)
    ___ On occasion, usually while in church (2)
    ___ During personal devotions two or more times a week (3)
    ___ During daily devotions, consistent Bible study, and meditation (4)

25. I look forward to memorizing and meditating on God's Word:
    ___ Never (1)
    ___ Rarely (2)
    ___ On occasion (3)
    ___ Frequently (4)
    ___ Daily (5)

26. I engage in meaningful fellowship with other believers where we study the Scriptures and pray together:
    ___ Never (1)
    ___ Rarely (2)
    ___ Occasionally (3)
    ___ Regularly (every month, every other week, or weekly) (4)

27. My thought life is honoring to God:
    ___ Never (1)
    ___ Rarely (2)
    ___ Occasionally (3)
    ___ For the most part (4)

28. I am motivated to live righteously because:
  ___ I'm afraid that if I don't I'll go to hell (1)
  ___ I'm afraid the pastor and members of my church will reject me if I don't (2)
  ___ It's healthy for me (3)
  ___ I love God (4)

29. Sharing my faith in Christ with another is:
  ___ Repugnant to me (1)
  ___ Shaming to me (2)
  ___ Fearful to me (3)
  ___ A duty to me (4)
  ___ A joy to me (5)

Spiritual Health Score: _____

25-31	Good
18-24	Fair
Less than 18	Poor

Physical Health Score: _____
Mental and Emotional Health Score: _____
Social Health Score: _____
Spiritual Health Score: _____

If you're like most people, you probably scored lower in at least one category than you did in the others. For example, when I (Randy) took the quiz, I discovered that although I'm doing fairly well in most areas, I need to work on my physical health. I eat too much junk food, I don't get enough regular exercise, and consequently I'm overweight.

Don't feel too bad if you, too, found you need work in one or more areas. The quiz isn't meant to make you feel guilty but to show you where you can improve your health, so try to look at it from that perspective. On the other hand, don't be complacent if you scored fair or below in just one category, thinking you're fine as you are. (If you scored high in the good range in every category, are you sure you were being honest?) Remember that all our three parts are interrelated, so if you're not where you ought to be in just one area, it will drag down your overall health.

That's a brief description of what whole-person health looks like. Now we're ready to move into part 2 of this book, where we consider what usually goes wrong with our health. As we'll see in the next chapter, the same basic problems affect every area of life.

TO YOUR HEALTH

1. Do you agree that "while pain is inevitable, misery is not"? Why or why not?

2. Based on the description of whole-person health given in this chapter, who would you say is the healthiest person you know? Why?

3. If you haven't already done so, take the health self-test that makes up the latter part of this chapter. Based on the results, in what area do you have the greatest need for improvement? Why?

4. What can you do, starting today or tomorrow, to begin increasing your health in that area?

Part 2

What Usually Goes Wrong

4

WHERE OUR TROUBLES BEGIN

Phil was a memorable patient of ours. He had started and run his own business, but he couldn't make it work financially, and eventually the business failed. When that happens, naturally, there's a lot of emotional pain. Perhaps you or someone you know can identify with that kind of setback.

In Phil's case, the pain of failure was more severe because Phil believed that someone else had "done him wrong" and was therefore responsible for the loss of his business. Thus Phil had to face interpersonal conflict as well as a financial setback and the resulting blow to his self-esteem.

Phil could have chosen to deal with his pain in a healthy manner. We all have that option. But he chose an unhealthy way instead. He chose to become bitter. He determined to get revenge against the person who had mistreated him—even to the point of wanting to commit murder. This bitterness took a heavy toll on Phil. He grew depressed and despondent to such an extent that he no longer wanted to live, and he seriously considered suicide.

Eventually, we're happy to report, Phil did come into the hospital, and we had a chance to talk with him. After some time and considerable effort, we convinced him to choose to love the person he was bitter toward, and they finally resolved their differences. But all this healing took place only after Phil had suffered a lot of unnecessary pain and distance from others.

No Respecter of Persons

Phil's story illustrates one of the key problems in maintaining whole-person health. Namely, while pain of various kinds is an inevitable part of this life, our natural human tendency is to try to avoid it. We may displace the pain onto someone else, as Phil did, or use another of the methods outlined in the next chapter. But however we do it, we try to avoid everything from the pain of exercise and of denying ourselves that second piece of cake in the physical realm to the pain involved in reconciling a broken relationship and the pain of admitting our absolute dependence upon God. And in attempting to avoid pain or anesthetize it with alcohol or some other drug, we get ourselves into great physical, emotional, and spiritual trouble.

Remember, as whole people we operate in three dimensions: body, mind, and spirit. As shown in Figure 4, each part affects the other two, and the others affect it. Physical pain ignored will pop up to affect our mind and spirit. Similarly, avoiding any spiritual pain (bitterness toward God, for example) eventually will cause that pain to spill over into the mental or physical areas of life. We do not always recognize the impact of ignoring our pain. In fact, we often resent having pain in our lives. As psychiatrist Scott Peck wrote in *The Road Less Traveled*,

> Most do not fully see this truth that life is difficult. Instead they moan more or less incessantly, noisily or subtly, about the enormity of their problems, their burdens, and their difficulties as if life were generally easy, as if life should be easy. They voice their belief, noisily or subtly, that their difficulties represent a unique kind of affliction that should not be and that has somehow been especially visited upon them, or else upon their families, their tribe, their class, their nation, their race or even their species, and not upon others.[1]

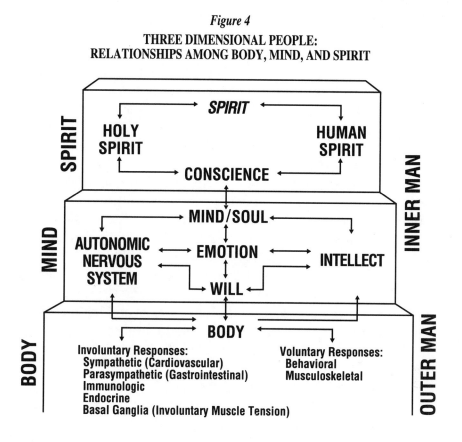

Figure 4

**THREE DIMENSIONAL PEOPLE:
RELATIONSHIPS AMONG BODY, MIND, AND SPIRIT**

Those of us who are not wealthy are tempted to think that a pile of money solves most of life's problems. No doubt it makes life easier in some ways. But the wealthy are hardly exempt from suffering, either. As Jack Lemmon, the highly successful and very-well-paid actor, once said, "Like a lot of people, I used to think success meant having money or fame. And I figured it ended all your problems. It doesn't. They just change. You get some new problems just as big."

The desire to deny the inevitability of pain has even given rise to a line of Christian theology that says it is God's intention for us to enjoy pain-free lives. Christians need only have sufficient faith and God will gladly banish their pain, illness, or disease. This "name it and claim it" theology has caused a great deal of false guilt and confusion. Contrary to the sincere yet misguided belief of such Christian teaching, suffering is an inevitable part of human life. Recognizing and accepting that fact is the first step in dealing with it in a healthy way.

God allows pain and suffering. He always has. Consider just three modern occurrences. A loving, giving Christian couple in their seventies are rocked when the husband has a stroke and lies in a nursing home bed, unable to swallow. A wonderful Christian mother who had many health problems as a child prays fervently that her own daughter will be spared such agony. Yet when the girl is four years old, she also begins to experience painful illnesses that her doctors struggle to understand. Why would a loving God allow these things to occur? A hard-working, Christian man follows what he believes to be God's leading in opening his own roofing company. Yet after just a short time, the business goes bankrupt, and the man and his family are left with a ruined credit rating and a sizable debt they feel honor-bound to repay. Where is God in this situation?

Whether you have little faith or great faith, suffering may come. Consider the stalwart apostle Paul. He once described his experiences this way: "To this very hour we go hungry and thirsty, we are in rags, we are brutally treated, we are homeless. . . . Up to this moment we have become the scum of the earth, the refuse of the world (1 Corinthians 4:11, 13).

Another time he described himself as having been

> exposed to death again and again. Five times I received from
> the Jews the forty lashes minus one. Three times I was beaten
> with rods, once I was stoned, three times I was shipwrecked, I
> spent a night and a day in the open sea. . . . I have been in
> danger from rivers, in danger from bandits. . . . I have labored
> and toiled and have often gone without sleep; . . . I have been
> cold and naked. Besides everything else, I face daily my con-
> cern for all the churches" (2 Corinthians 11: 23-28).

Did Paul lack the faith needed to experience God's deliv-
erance and provision? Hardly. Did he simply fail to pray about
his needs? How absurd! Just a little later in 2 Corinthians, he
described a thorn in the flesh given to him to keep him humble,
and he added,

> Three times I pleaded with the Lord to take it away from me.
> But he said to me, "My grace is sufficient for you, for my power
> is made perfect in weakness." Therefore I will boast all the
> more gladly about my weaknesses, so that Christ's power may
> rest on me. That is why, for Christ's sake, I delight in weak-
> nesses, in insults, in hardships, in persecutions, in difficulties.
> For when I am weak, then I am strong (12:8-10).

That's a far cry from a "name it and claim it" theology, isn't
it? As author Stephen Brown puts it, "The Bible never teaches that
we won't suffer, or that we will always be happy. The Bible teaches power under pressure, not power without pressure."[2]

Here's a little more of what the Bible teaches: "Dear
friends, do not be surprised at the painful trial you are suffering,
as though something strange were happening to you" (1 Peter
4:12). "In this world you will have trouble. But take heart! I [Je-
sus] have overcome the world" (John 16:33). "If anyone would
come after me [Jesus], he must deny himself and take up his
cross daily and follow me" (Luke 9:23). That is not an invitation
to a bed of roses. We'll say much more about this subject in
chapter 8. For now, let's recognize that much of our pain cannot

be avoided and should not be ignored. When we try to ignore or deny our pain, we will suffer a breakdown in whole-person health. In effect, a breakdown in communication occurs among the parts of our being.

ILLNESS: A BREAKDOWN IN COMMUNICATION

Whenever whole-person health suffers, we probably will have a breakdown in communication. This applies to illness in any of our three parts, as well as to the spreading of the effects of that sickness into the other two parts.

In a healthy human body, for example, good communication within individual cells, between cells, and between organs assures that everything works properly. Consider an adult's bronchial tubes—the tubes that feed oxygen to the lungs and carry away carbon dioxide. The cells in those tubes "talk" to each other and the brain so that just enough of them are made to replace the cells that die naturally from day to day.

But let's look at what happens in the bronchial tubes of a smoker. Regular smoking continually exposes the tubes to such injurious chemicals as nicotine, tar, carbon monoxide, and hydrocarbons. Over time, those chemicals may penetrate the wall of a cell in the tubes and transform the genetic material in the nucleus. Then, when a normal cell would stop reproducing because enough cells have been made, that message no longer gets through to this cell, and it keeps reproducing, out of control. A cancer is born.

If things work the way they're supposed to, the person's immune system will recognize the excess cells as invaders and respond by sending white blood cells to kill them. But if the immune system is impaired for some reason—perhaps a great stress or traumatic illness—the cancer may grow big enough to overwhelm the system's ability to keep it in check. The renegade cells can't be killed fast enough.

If the growth continues, several very dangerous things may happen. The cancer may become large enough to block off the tube and begin to suffocate the person. It may secrete fluid that builds up in the lung, blocking the intake of oxygen and exhalation of carbon dioxide and literally drowning the person. Or a few cancer cells may break away and be carried to another part of the body, such as the spinal cord or the brain, starting out-of-control growth there (a process called metastasizing).

All this deadly activity begins with chemically induced miscommunication within and between a few microscopic cells, and it will eventually have enormous impact on every part of the person, for the body, mind, and spirit are inseparable.

WITHIN THE BODY

All diseases originated in the fall of the human race back in the Garden of Eden. God had designed a perfect world without illness, but with the advent of sin came death and the diseases that cause it. We read in Romans 8: "The creation was subjected to frustration, not by its own choice. . . . We know that the whole creation has been groaning as in the pains of childbirth right up to the present time" (vv. 20, 22). And again, physical disease comes from some communication breakdown within the body.

Just one change in a tiny gene inside a DNA molecule, for instance, can cause a different chemical to be produced from the one a healthy body produces. Sickle-cell anemia, for example, is an inherited illness caused by a single incorrect "letter" in the 60,000-letter gene producing hemoglobin, a protein that carries oxygen in the blood and gives blood its red color. That flawed part of the gene mistakenly tells the whole to manufacture hemoglobin that cannot bind normally to oxygen. The hemoglobin molecule becomes severely contorted as oxygen leaves the red blood cells; the usually smooth, donut-shaped cells transform into crescent or sickle-shaped blood cells. These fragile, deformed red blood cells have one of three fates. They break apart in the blood stream, get "gobbled up" by the spleen in an effort to remove the abnormal cells, or they clump together in a "sludge," clogging the small vessels or vital organs.

The result for the victim is chronic anemia, fever, terrible abdominal and joint pains, jaundice, and early death. All this from a biochemical miscommunication, one incorrect "letter" in the gene that manufactures hemoglobin. At present, there is no cure for this killer.

Another example of genetic miscommunication is found in the lungs. A normal lung cell produces a chemical called alpha one antitrypsin, and it helps the lungs to secrete mucus and stay open so they can breathe properly. But if one mistaken gene puts out miscommunication about which chemical to produce, the result will be a deficiency of alpha one antitrypsin, and emphysema (chronic lung disease) will develop. Fortunately, in the case of this disease, we've been able to isolate the chemical, and doctors can now give their patients alpha one antitrysin and reverse their emphysema.

One of the most exciting new developments in medicine, in fact, is this process of treating genetic illness by introducing genetic material into the body that will cause normal interaction to begin to take place within the cells. A recent article in *U. S. News & World Report* told of the first human trial of gene therapy.

The patient was a four-year-old girl suffering from a rare, inherited disease in which a genetic defect cripples the immune system, leaving the victim open to every kind of infection. "To treat it, her doctors removed immune cells from her blood, fitted them with a new gene, and reinjected them into her body." And four months after her last dose of the correctly coded genes, at the time the article was written, "the girl's immune system appears to be fending off infections normally."[3]

Now consider what happens when someone suffers a stroke and one side of the body is paralyzed, as often occurs. We know that the right side of the brain largely controls the left side of the body (and vice versa). It does that by sending signals through the nerves—communication—to the muscles that produce movement. In simple terms, then, when a stroke damages the right side of the brain, it may hinder, if not block completely, the brain's ability to communicate with the muscles on the body's left side. Thus the paralysis.

Communication also takes place between organs in the body by means of nerves, hormones, and chemicals that are released by one organ and then bind onto the cells of another and tell it what to do. The pituitary gland, for example, secretes a number of hormones that stimulate and regulate bodily functions, among them overall growth of the body.

This kind of communication within the body is the most elementary level of functioning. It is carried out in all animals by the brain stem, that primitive part of the brain at the top of the spinal cord that maintains basic bodily functions and so keeps us alive. In the lowest forms of animal life, that's all the brain function they have.

As you climb the ladder of complexity in the animal kingdom, you come next to those animals that also have a limbic system sitting atop the brain stem. You'll recall from chapter 2 that the limbic brain has to do with emotions. Thus an animal at this level, such as a reptile, has the ability to experience very basic emotions like fear and rage. God gave such animals that ability for their protection, so they can respond to threats in their environment, such as from predators.

WITHIN THE MIND

The most complex forms of communication reside within people. Among God's creation, the human brain is the most sophisticated communication system. In addition to the brain stem and limbic system, we have a highly developed cerebral cortex with which we can reason, remember, develop concepts, and communicate them in symbolic language. This ability makes us unique in God's creation.

Our capacity for reflecting on the past helps to protect us, to keep us from making the same mistakes over and over. But more importantly, it allows us to commune with Him who is the Word and to bring Him glory as we consider what He's done in creation and in our lives and the lives of others. Further, our ability to anticipate the distant future, which no animal can come close to, enables us to know innately that the Creator

God has provided a life beyond the physical, beyond death, toward which we're all heading.

The human brain is truly amazing in its complexity. One eminent professor of neurobiology estimated that it would take researchers billions of years to fully understand it. A single human brain contains 100 billion nerve cells; that's the number of stars there are in the Andromeda galaxy. And each of those cells has one thousand synapses (connections to other cells).[4] Altogether, the number of synapses in one brain is ten to the fourteenth power. That's 100 trillion connections between cells! It's just incredible, and it's all so we can communicate with others and with God.

With all those cells and connections, there's also great potential for miscommunication within the brain. It often happens when we use defense mechanisms to cover up our pain (more about them in chapter 5) and end up believing lies. The brain stem, limbic system, basal ganglia, and most of the cerebral cortex function at a subconscious level. That's the level at which defense mechanisms occur in the effort to block painful memories and emotions from our conscious awareness.

Sally, twenty-eight, was hospitalized with extreme depression and assorted physical ailments. She was physically ill with a lack of energy, a marked loss of appetite, and a persistent "knot" in her stomach. Sally had no idea why she felt depressed. In working with her at length, we discovered that when she was twelve years old her dad had walked out on her and her mother.

As he left, Sally had cried from the top of the stairs, "Dad, don't leave! Dad, don't leave!" She had worshiped the man, but he had walked out of her life forever.

Sally had denied the impact that event had on her, refusing to acknowledge the significance of his leaving to her young heart and mind. In fact, she had blocked the pain out of her mind; she covered up the truth and went on.

Now, years later, the painful truth bubbled up in emotional depression and physical sickness. As we explored that and opened her mind to the truth of painful memories, she admitted her tendency to deny what had happened and how that had hurt her. Gradually, over a long period, she accepted the truth and cleared the lines of communication between her body and her emotions.

Similarly, Alzheimer's disease initially affects the mind, but its impact can influence behavior and emotions as well. Although Alzheimer's is receiving much attention these days, researchers still are uncertain what causes it. We do know that it destroys the brain cells essential to memory, emotions, and thought. The result is loss of short-term memory, abnormal—sometimes even violent—behavior, and often reversion to a childlike emotional state.

BETWEEN PEOPLE

Good interaction is also crucial between people. The lack of it kills relationships. In his book *Communication: Key to Your Marriage*, counselor Norm Wright says, "The number one problem in marriage is poor communication. Marriage is an intimate relationship built on mutual understanding, but in order to truly understand another person you must be able to communicate with him. A husband and wife can know a great deal about each other without really knowing one another."[5]

Betty could not communicate with her husband, who was emotionally cold and distant. He would not open to her at all. Unfortunately, she also did not choose to make the best of the situation, realizing his limitations. Neither did she choose to communicate with other women in a healthy way to have her need for fellowship at least partially met.

Eventually, Betty completely blocked communication with her husband by having an extramarital affair, which intensified the whole situation. Finally she came in for counseling.

She was extremely depressed—in fact, on the verge of being psychotic (losing touch with reality). We began to work with Betty to open up the lines of communication between her and her husband. As he became more aware of her deep and legitimate needs, as she realized she could not control him, and as they learned some basic communication skills, they gradually rebuilt their marriage, and her depression began to lift.

We've all heard numerous stories about a person saying and meaning one thing, thinking the message was perfectly clear, and the hearer understanding the speaker to be saying something entirely different. Perhaps you've played the party game in which the first person whispers a short message to the second, who passes it to the third, and so on down the line until the last person repeats the message out loud. By then, the message has usually been distorted beyond recognition! That's a simple but clear illustration of the important truth that, while we have a tremendous capacity for communication, getting a point across can still be extremely difficult, especially when the subject is sensitive. We all tend to hear what we want to hear. But the result of a failure to communicate can be disaster, as in Betty's case.

Such a marriage is an obvious example of the harm that can be done to relationships by poor communication. But the same truth applies to all relationships—within a family, in a church, in the workplace, or wherever people live, work, worship, and play together.

BETWEEN US AND GOD

Spiritual disease is also a breakdown in communication, this time between us and God. Isaiah 59:2 declares, "But your iniquities have separated you from your God; your sins have hidden his face from you, so that he will not hear." When we're in a state of sin, refusing to surrender some sin or control of some area of our lives to Him, our ability to commune with Him in prayer is gone. That's spiritual illness.

Fortunately, by God's grace, there is a cure for this kind of sickness. Those who have never established communication with God can do so by acknowledging they are sinners (see Romans 3:23) and believing in Jesus Christ as their Savior from sin (see Romans 6:23; 10:9-10). Those who are already Chris-

tians can confess their sins with the assurance that He will forgive and cleanse (see 1 John 1:9).

But there's also another kind of spiritual sickness, a
breakdown in communication between us and God that arises
by our own choice. This happens when we develop doubts
about God's care or His ability to answer our prayers. In his
book *Disappointment with God*, Philip Yancey explains it well:

> I have found that petty disappointments tend to accumulate
> over time, undermining my faith with a lava flow of doubt. I
> start to wonder whether God cares about everyday details—
> about me. I am tempted to pray less often, having concluded in
> advance that it won't matter. Or will it? My emotions and my
> faith waver. Once those doubts seep in, I am even less pre-
> pared for times of major crisis. A neighbor is dying of cancer; I
> pray diligently for her. But even as I pray, I wonder. Can God be
> trusted? If so many small prayers go unanswered, what about
> the big ones?[6]

For that kind of doubt that makes us hesitant to reach out
to God, there is no simple answer. But there is a healthy
approach. Pastor and author Bill Hybels summarizes it this
way:

> When [we're doubtful or disappointed], we need to acknowl-
> edge our gut-level responses. We need to admit to ourselves
> that we're afraid, lonely, disappointed, or angry.
>
> The second step is to honestly tell God how we feel. He
> can handle our authentic cries of pain and disappointment. He
> can even help us work through them. . . .
>
> What I've learned is that often these authentic outpour-
> ings of frustration, or even anger, are necessary steps on the
> path to wholeness. The cathartic process of pouring our hearts
> out to the Lord, of emptying ourselves of pent-up emotions and
> unanswered questions, opens the way for insight and
> understanding.
>
> The same thing happens to us that so often happened to
> the psalmist. After the outburst comes the renewed perspec-
> tive. The lights go on. We realize anew that in spite of the

heartache or the unanswered questions, God is still God. There is still hope. We still matter to Him. The Holy Spirit still lives in us. The Bible is still true. The church is still intact. Heaven still awaits. And in that we can rejoice.[7]

The key, then, is to just keep talking to the Lord. We can be brutally honest with Him without fear. No one hears us better; no one loves us more.

We've seen now how our troubles begin while seeking to be healthy, whole people. And one of the keys we explored is our desire to deny the reality of pain in our lives. That wish leads in turn to some very common but extremely unhealthy ways of handling the pain. In the next chapter, we look more closely at those unsatisfying and even harmful methods. You may even recognize yourself or your loved ones in one of the descriptions.

To Your Health

1. What can happen if we ignore pain for a long time?

2. Is there some pocket of pain you know you've been trying to avoid? If so, what is it?

3. How have you talked to God about the pain in your life? How has He seemed to respond?

4. What are some keys to maintaining good communication within your body? Between yourself and others?

5

 "IT'S ALL HER FAULT!"

I don't think I've had a heart attack. Maybe it's some sort of heart disease," Jan explained when she came to our office. At age thirty-five, she had "a little rapid heartbeat," as she called it. From that had grown the certainty that she was the victim of one heart disease or another.

We admitted her to the hospital and did every available heart test—EKG, treadmill, echocardiogram, and so on. All the tests turned up negative. We simply could not find any trace of heart disease. Nonetheless, Jan remained obsessed with the idea that something was seriously wrong with her heart.

Because we couldn't find any physical problem, we turned our attention to other possible causes of Jan's tremendous anxiety. After some time of talking with her and examining her past, we found two things to be at the root of her fear about her heart.

First, she had some deep-seated anxiety from her childhood that she had never dealt with. "My parents divorced when I was just a little girl," Jan said, and she admitted to feeling insecure ever since. "I just can't trust others; at some point they might leave me too. I never have felt safe in any relationship."

Second, Jan's husband had suffered some financial setbacks in recent years, creating further anxiety in her mind. "The two big questions I have are: Will we pay our bills? Can we someday lose everything?" Jan had no peace of mind about their financial future.

Our conclusion was that Jan had displaced both of those fears into anxiety about her heart. That was really a decoy that allowed her to dwell on something other than her real concerns.

As we said in the previous chapter, the natural human tendency is to try to avoid the pain in our lives, and that's exactly what Jan was doing. It's a very common reaction, and it's one of the biggest obstacles to whole-person health. After all, you can't deal with a problem until you understand and admit you have it in the first place. So in this chapter, we will look at twenty-five ways people try—usually without even realizing it— to avoid harsh reality. We see these methods frequently during counseling. You might recognize yourself in one or more of them if you read the descriptions honestly and prayerfully.

FROM THE BEGINNING

People have been trying to avoid life's pain from the very beginning of human experience. Adam and Eve were created out of God's love because He wanted intimate, honest, and unbroken fellowship with them. They were put in a perfect place and told to be fruitful and multiply. And then came the deceiver and the fall forever from innocence of the human race (see Genesis 1: 27-31; 3:1-23).

After Adam and Eve sinned, notice what happened. "Then the eyes of both of them were opened, and they realized they were naked; so they sewed fig leaves together and made coverings for themselves" (Genesis 3:7).

Before, they had been completely honest with their Creator. The thought had never even entered their minds that they should cover their bodies from His sight. They had no need or desire to hide anything. But now they were lawbreakers, and they knew it, and they were ashamed. They felt great mental, emotional, and spiritual pain. And a common reaction of those who feel shame is to try to cover up their wrongdoing, to bury the pain. What our original father and mother started continues to this day. We continue to cover up our wrongdoings, our failures, and our perceived inadequacies.

Adam and Eve then heard the Lord walking in the garden, and how did they respond? No longer did they run joyously to meet Him. Instead, "they hid from the Lord God among the trees of the garden" (v. 8). When God asked Adam where he was, Adam replied, "I heard you in the garden, and I was afraid because I was naked; so I hid" (v. 10). Adam was feeling guilty in addition to his shame, afraid of God's displeasure because of his sin. So he tried to hide from the lawmaker, even as people do today.

Hiding didn't work, though, and soon enough, God confronted Adam and Eve's sin. "Have you eaten from the tree that I commanded you not to eat from?" He asked Adam directly (v. 11).

How did Adam respond? Did he face the problem, admit his failure, and seek God's forgiveness? No, he tried to shift the blame—twice in one sentence. "The woman you put here with me—she gave me some fruit from the tree, and I ate it" (v. 12). It was all Eve's fault, he suggested. She picked the forbidden fruit—something he never would have done, of course—and gave it to him. And how was he supposed to turn her down without hurting her feelings? So he ate. Like a kid caught throwing the second punch in a fight, he pointed at her and said, in effect, "She started it!"

But that was only one shot at shifting the blame for his sin. Notice how he said, "The woman *you* put here with me" (our emphasis). In other words, he implied, when you got right down to it, that the whole problem was really God's fault! Talk about passing the buck!

What all this shows is that when we try to shift the blame for our failures, we aren't coming up with anything new. Human beings typically choose to avoid blame by assigning it to someone or something else. But we are not fooling God, even if we manage to pull the wool over the eyes of others; He's been hearing that line for thousands of years, since Adam set the pattern.

Hiding, trying to cover up, and shifting the blame or inventing some other excuse have at least one thing in common: they are conscious, deliberate efforts to avoid conflict and pain. But much of the time, our attempts are unconscious, almost automatic responses to life's difficulties and our personal shortcomings. The technical term for these responses is defense mechanisms. We defend ourselves against accepting our responsibilities (see Figure 5).

The clearest biblical statement of this phenomenon is found in Jeremiah 17:9: "The heart is deceitful above all things and beyond cure. Who can understand it?" In other words, from God's point of view, defense mechanisms are a form of self-deception that gives us a false sense of protection. Although we may not be aware of what we're doing, He sees right through us: "I the Lord search the heart and examine the mind, to reward a man according to his conduct, according to what his deeds deserve" (Jeremiah 17:10).

In our quest for health, then, we can be assured that God understands not only our pain, but also our instinctive ways of responding that only delay real healing. Not only does He understand, but He has also promised to stick with us and work in us as we grow toward wellness: "We can be confident of this, that he who began a good work in you will carry it on to completion until the day of Jesus Christ" (Philippians 1:6). That vital promise can help us to desire change and accept responsibility for that change. (We'll say more about the process of getting and staying healthy in chapters 8 and 9.)

With that in mind, here are some common defense mechanisms people use to avoid pain. As you read about them, realize that you probably will recognize one or more that you use regularly to some extent. Of course, those will be areas you will want to work on. But realize also that you are not alone: almost every person uses at least one defense mechanism to some extent. It's part of what it means to live in a fallen world. Alas, none of the devices can deliver us from pain; they can only delay it.

Figure 5
THE ORIGINAL DEFENSE MECHANISMS

<u>Adam's Spiritual Emotions</u>   <u>Defense Mechanisms</u>

<u>Shame:</u> Loss of self-esteem
when the law-breaker fails to ─────────→ **1. COVER-UP**
live up to the requirements of
the Law-maker.

<u>Guilt:</u> Fear of abandonment
by the Law-maker when the ─────────→ **2. HIDING**
law-breaker fails to live up to
the requirements of the Law-maker.

                              3. BLAME-SHIFTING

The three defense mechanisms came in response to the
painful spiritual emotions of shame and guilt.

HIDING OUR PAIN

What happened in the Garden of Eden was only the beginning of human attempts to deny difficult reality. In the millenia since, our minds have devised numerous defensive strategies to protect ourselves. Below are twenty-five that show up again and again. Obviously, we could say a lot more about each one, but we've kept our descriptions brief to give a simple, quick introduction to each.

1. *Denial*. In people who practice denial, their thoughts, feelings, wishes, or motives are denied access to consciousness. These people will continue to deny sincerely their sinfulness, even when it has become obvious to everyone around them.

A good example is a provocative, flamboyant woman who behaves seductively but isn't aware of doing so and denies that her actions are provoking a response. She then becomes angry at the man for making sexually suggestive responses.

2. *Distortion*. Those who practice distortion grossly reshape external reality to suit their inner needs, frequently including grandiose delusions, wish-fulfilling delusions, and hallucinations (for example, "voices from God"). In many cases, however, the recasting of reality is more subtle and not so obvious.

An example of distortion was Sam, an extremely insecure man who was failing courses in medical school. To protect himself from the pain of that reality, Sam convinced himself that he would soon be asked to become president of the school because of his great insights. He also "heard" God's voice several times per hour, reassuring him of his delusions.

3. *Delusional projection*. Sometimes people are so afraid of their own feelings, perhaps anger or lust, that they project their feelings (like a slide on a screen) onto others around them. Such a person convinces himself that those other people possess the feelings and are plotting to use the feelings against him.

King Saul, the first king of Israel, was a good example of this. Unaware of his own jealousy and hatred toward David, King Saul developed the delusion that David was trying to kill him. The king projected his own murderous intentions onto David, accusing the young man of plotting to kill him.

4. *Primary projection*. This is the same as delusional projection but not of such psychotic (out of touch with reality) proportions. Nearly everyone uses primary projection, and it is the primary defense mechanism of paranoid personalities.

For example, Bob craves attention, but he is unaware of it because the knowledge would hurt his false pride. Being around others who seek attention raises his anxiety (fear of finding out the truth) level, so he self-righteously condemns them instead of facing his desires.

5. *Introjection*. The opposite of projection; people symbolically redirect toward themselves the feelings they have about another person or the feelings of the other individual. They turn the emotion inward, damaging themselves. Consider a compulsive person who may feel angry at another. To avoid feeling guilty about the anger, he "introjects" it toward himself. Similarly, a counselor may assume the depression of a patient, thinking that by taking on such suffering, she will somehow relieve the counselee. In reality, both leave the session feeling painfully sad.

6. *Schizoid fantasy*. People who use this defense escape the pain of reality through excessive daydreaming.

Shy and fearful of intimacy, Janet spent a lot of time in schizoid fantasy about the perfect romance. She refused to date the boys who asked her out, because they didn't measure up to the perfect man of her dreams. She even became angry at God for not providing her with a mate, when she was actually unconsciously rejecting all men.

7. *Isolation*. People who use this mechanism split off unacceptable emotions (for example, jealousy, greed, or lust) and isolate them from conscious awareness. This mechanism is commonly used by compulsive individuals whose consciences are so strict that they mistakenly think all anger is sin. They isolate their anger to relieve their false guilt. Instead, they should become aware of their anger, deal with their problems maturely, and reconcile with those who have made them angry.

8. *Rationalization.* In this common defense against pain and conflict, people justify unacceptable attitudes, beliefs, or behavior by the misapplication of justifying reasons or the invention of false reasons.

Jerry spends an inordinate amount of time with a female coworker because of lustful thoughts toward her; yet he excuses this time by convincing himself his motives are pure. Jerry rationalizes his seeing her as an act of Christian love. "She needs extensive time with a father figure to compensate for her own father, who ignored her as a child," Jerry says. His explanation denies and distorts his true motive.

9. *Reaction formation.* Those who use this mechanism adopt attitudes and behaviors that are the opposite of their true conscious or unconscious impulses.

One example would be a religious leader who harbors strong sexual urges and becomes an evangelist, preaching primarily against sexual promiscuity and sex education in the schools.

10. *Repression.* In this defense, unacceptable feelings, impulses, or ideas are banished from conscious awareness or prevented from coming into awareness. Everyone uses repression to some extent; it is the primary defense mechanism on which all others are based.

John, a Christian dying of cancer, continually repressed his anger toward God. Later he felt insulted when a close friend asked John if his anger had caused him to lose interest in having personal devotions. John was seemingly unaware that he was angry toward God and became offended when someone tried to point out the anger.

11. *Unhealthy suppression.* People who use suppression indefinitely postpone dealing with conscious conflict. They suppress the truth by convincing themselves they will take care of it later, but later never comes. This is actually a semiconscious defense mechanism.

The men and women Paul described in Romans 1:18-32 illustrate suppression. "The wrath of God is being revealed from heaven against all the godlessness and wickedness of men who suppress the truth by their wickedness. . . . They are gossips, slanderers, God-haters, insolent, arrogant, and boastful; they invent ways of doing evil; they disobey their parents" (vv. 18, 29-30). They incurred the wrath of God because they suppressed the truth about their sinfulness and need of a savior, becoming steadily more sinful as a result.

12. *Phariseeism.* In this case, people grow increasingly self-righteous to avoid becoming aware of their own depravity. Their words and often their actions suggest a devotion to God, but they speak and act righteously in an effort to avoid dealing with their sinful actions and attitudes done in private.

An example would be a young man we'll call Mike. Mike has unconscious inferiority feelings and recognizes his sins. To avoid focusing on them, he decides to complete seminary and become a preacher. Eventually he becomes a pastor, feeding his congregation a constant diet of legalism. Mike thinks he's more righteous than less-legalistic Christians and loves to make a show of his "spirituality."

13. *Defensive devaluation.* This mechanism is related to Phariseeism and projection. Individuals continually criticize others to convince themselves they are better. Almost everyone uses this to cover up unconscious feelings of inferiority. People who use it frequently are angry at themselves for not being perfect, and they key on the imperfections of others who remind them of their own shortcomings.

14. *Passive-aggressive unconscious behavior.* In this instance, passive people who have repressed hostility toward an individual or institution on which they're dependent get unconscious revenge in nonverbal ways, such as pouting, procrastination, stubbornness, inefficiency, or obstructionism.

Stan, an alcoholic, represses his hostility toward a domineering, compulsive wife. He doesn't dare express his anger or even become aware of it, so he gets even by coming home late from work and putting off daily chores. And he drinks regularly. Stan's actions mainly harm himself; eventually he will die of liver disease.

15. *Withdrawal*. Some people deceive themselves about the existence of tension-producing conflict by removing themselves from the situation.

For example, Hal is an introvert who fears intimacy and rejection but denies that fear to himself. As a result, he has been engaged three times but has withdrawn from each relationship when the marriage approached, not realizing the true reason.

16. *Displacement*. People who use this defense "displace," or transfer, an emotion from its original object to a more acceptable substitute.

George, for instance, is angry at his boss but afraid to be aware of it. When he goes home, he criticizes his wife for minor things or spanks his child for something he would normally ignore. Similarly, one five-year-old with intense feelings of love for her father wants to marry him when she grows up. She can't now, so she displaces her love to her teddy bear and takes it everywhere she goes. Though her innocent love is not harmful, it can set a pattern for a lifetime of displaced feelings.

17. *Regression*. In regression, individuals faced with conflict return to an earlier stage of emotional immaturity where they felt protected from life's stresses.

Billy has an infant brother who makes him uncomfortable. Billy, age four, has unconscious conflicts about his mother's being in the hospital for a week and then spending much of her time with the baby. Though he is toilet-trained, Billy suddenly regresses to bed wetting, baby talk, soiling his pants, temper tantrums, and hyperactivity. He doesn't know why and even is embarrassed at times. But unconsciously, he is hoping that by returning to infancy, when he had all his mother's attention, he will again receive her individual care.

18. *Somatization*. This fancy word simply means that unacceptable feelings (like anger) or motives (such as vengeance) are represented by physical symptoms (headaches, diarrhea, or heartburn, for example) in parts of the body regulated by the autonomic (involuntary) nervous system. The people keep their minds on their physical symptoms to avoid being aware of their true feelings and motives. Most of us use this

mechanism regularly to one extent or another; some, like hypochondriacs, use it excessively. Back in chapter 2, Suzy Morgan's headache and upset stomach were largely the result of her anxiety about feeling out of control and because of her anger toward her insensitive, demanding boss.

19. *Unhealthy sublimation.* People using this defense channel consciously unacceptable drives into acceptable expressions, never even becoming aware that the unacceptable drives exist.

A boy grows up in a cold, critical, hostile, but strictly religious family. Being aware of his own hostile drives would hurt his pride and conscience, so he becomes an expert hunter as a boy, then a football middle linebacker known for his "killer instinct," and finally a surgeon who cuts people's bodies to save their lives. Such behavior outwardly seems positive, for the person may be acquiring skills and has incentive for constructive behavior. However, he is motivated by negative reasons, and he never deals with his anger toward his family.

20. *Compensation.* Some individuals unconsciously try to make up for real or imagined personal deficiencies in physique, performance, talents, or psychological attributes. Their feelings of inferiority result from a lack of acceptance of the way God made them. Compensation can become a healthy defense if it's done consciously and with proper motives.

Heidi, age sixteen, decides to apply lots of makeup and become sexually active. Heidi believes she is unattractive and is trying to compensate for her insecure feelings, though she does not realize this is her motive.

21. *Sarcasm.* People with repressed hostility toward themselves, others, or a group may ventilate that hostility without even being aware of its existence, by making critical jokes about themselves or others.

An illustration is a man who has much repressed hostility toward his mother and women in general. He makes up constant critical jokes about the supposed ignorance or inferiority of women and doesn't understand why some people are offended by his "innocent sarcasm."

22. *Acting out*. An individual who is unaware of his unacceptable urges acts them out through such behaviors as sexual promiscuity or compulsive stealing.

A sadly all-too-common illustration is a teenage girl who feels totally ignored by her father. She represses her craving for his love and approval, then finds herself being promiscuous with boys who unconsciously remind her of him. She also compulsively steals things from males without knowing why; it's a symbolic way to steal her father's love.

23. *Intellectualization*. In this frequently used defense, people avoid becoming aware of their severe feelings of inferiority and other unconscious conflicts by the excessive use of intellectual vocabulary, discussions, and philosophies.

Scott grows up in a critical family. His grades are never good enough to satisfy his parents, leading him to develop feelings of inferiority. In college he becomes a philosophy major, uses lots of long, rarely used words, talks only about philosophical issues (never his own feelings), and looks down on people who are less intellectual than himself. Scott is avoiding the pain by adopting intellectualization as his defense.

24. *Hypochondriasis*. This is a more general defense than somatization. Here individuals convince themselves they are physically ill when they really aren't, or they exaggerate the severity of an illness they actually have.

An example would be a man who is lazy but nevertheless working to support his family. He develops a lower back problem and is laid up for six weeks, during which he is pampered, doesn't have to do anything responsible, and enjoys watching TV all day. Because of those many benefits, he unconsciously convinces himself he is still in terrible condition even after his back has healed completely.

25. *Controlling*. Insecure individuals who are relatively unaware of their feelings of severe powerlessness sometimes develop strong urges to think for and control others, thus causing themselves to feel more powerful.

Rob, a thirty-year-old engineer with a compulsive personality, almost had a nervous breakdown because of extreme insecurity and anxiety. He "fell in love" with a very dependent woman and controlled her totally in marriage, making nearly every decision for her. Thus he warded off some of his feelings of insecurity.

There you have a whirlwind tour through some of the common defense mechanisms we see in counseling. There are other defenses—more exotic and less common—yet just as counterproductive in dealing with interpersonal conflict and pain. For instance, a person trying to avoid unacceptable feelings or motives can have an *hysterical (histrionic) conversion reaction*, which causes a loss of function in a part of the body controlled by sensory or motor nerves. During the Vietnam War, many American soldiers experienced this defense, becoming paralyzed in one arm. It was noted that the affected arm was usually the man's primary shooting arm. Under hypnotism, the soldiers could use the arm, but it again became paralyzed when not under hypnosis.

Meanwhile, in *complex formation* several related or apparently unwanted ideas in the unconscious are associated in such a way that any environmental stimulus that threatens to bring one of them into conscious awareness will evoke the emotion associated with the entire group. Thus a young girl feels extreme anxiety when she is jumped on and bitten by a black dog. Later she represses the entire event. But as an adult, she develops extreme anxiety whenever a black cat crosses her path, and she wonders why.

We hope you have found this whirlwind tour interesting; you probably have recognized yourself and assorted acquaintances in some of the descriptions. Facing our unhealthy ways of dealing with life's pain is the first step in setting them aside and learning healthy alternatives that will enable us to get the most out of life, as God intends us to enjoy it.

As we continue to look at what usually goes wrong with whole-person health, we turn next to consider some of the false hopes that are nonetheless currently popular in the areas of physical and mental health. Some of these have been around a long time, and many come from the Far East. Some may even be partially valid.

TO YOUR HEALTH

1. In your own words, what is a defense mechanism?

   _____

   _____

   _____

2. Besides Adam, describe another biblical character who appeared to use a defense mechanism rather than face the truth.

3. Think of someone you know who has tried to avoid a hard reality. Which defense mechanism did that person use?

4. How did that person's friends and family respond?

5. How should a Christian respond to a person using a defense mechanism? Why? (For more on this, see chapter 10.)

6

FALSE HOPES FOR PHYSICAL HEALTH

A recent article in *Time* magazine told of a New York practitioner of several forms of alternative medicine: "Greer Jonas does reflexology with some aromatherapy thrown in. . . . Jonas works in her clean, well-lighted apartment. . . . Hanging crystals tinkle before an open window. Brown and blue bottles of lavender, rosemary and rose essence exude their fragrances. Lavender relaxes the client, Jonas advises. Rosemary 'breaks up fibrous tissue' when massaged into a woman's breasts."

Jonas, who has no medical degree, adds, "The body holds a lot of memories. . . . You touch an area, and sometimes the person starts to cry."[1]

More and more Americans are turning to alternative forms of medicine like those performed by Jonas, practices already accepted in other parts of the world, in their urgent quest for physical health. But as the same article notes, "The chief danger of alternative medicine—aside from wasting money—is that the patients get so carried away with unconventional cures that they dismiss regular medicine entirely."

Neurologist Clifford Saper of the University of Chicago concludes, "The nightmare . . . is seeing someone who has a spinal-cord tumor who's been going to a chiropractor for years instead of to a doctor. You want to throw your hands up and say, 'If only I'd seen him earlier I could have helped him that much more.' "[2]

A nationwide poll found that around 30 percent of the people surveyed have tried one kind of alternative treatment or another, half of them within the last year. It's now a $27 billion annual business, and it's growing steadily.

The quest for whole health of one's body, mind, and spirit takes people to many would-be curers, who practice a diverse set of therapies. What are these unusual forms of therapy on which so many people are pinning their hopes? What are they supposed to do, and what do we actually know about them? And why are so many people so willing to submit their minds and bodies to them? Those are the questions we want to answer in this chapter.

THE LURE OF THE UNUSUAL

On a superficial level, some people will always be drawn to the new and the faddish, even when it comes to how they care for their bodies. Many people are tired of the way conventional medicine is often practiced, with a series of specialists treating them like a collection of parts. And in some cases, people have tried all the usual approaches without success and are desperate for any kind of help.

But beyond those reasons are some deeper motivations that reflect the state of our culture and of human nature. One is the desire for a pain-free existence that we've talked about already. In one sense that desire is understandable, but the Bible also describes pain's ability to develop character in us and to make us utterly dependent on God, as we should be (see, for example, 2 Corinthians 12:7-10). Thus pain in itself is not bad. Its presence can even be beneficial. Shirley (see chapter 3) could teach us all a lot about that. Such a perspective, however, seems to be almost entirely missing today. Instead, when we experience any pain at all, we want relief, we want it *now*, and we don't care how we get it.

A second underlying motivation is our futile desire for eternal youthfulness. We spend tens of millions of dollars each year on creams and surgeries and spa treatments in our efforts to look forever twentysomething. Americans submit to procedures they know to be dangerous and even illegal, like facial silicone injections, to shed wrinkles and lines and the appearance of years. In times gone by, and still today in some cultures, gray hair was a sign of wisdom and maturity, a badge of respect. Not so in our youth-oriented society.

The ultimate goal, of course, is to live forever, and many people would like a way to achieve that without relying on the God revealed in the Bible. We'll say more about that in the next chapter.

AS OLD AS EGYPT

What are these alternative ways of caring for the body that are becoming so popular? We'll discuss a number of them, many of which have their roots in ancient Egypt, India, or China but now fall under the heading of New Age practices. Most are really on the fringes of medicine, with little or no scientific support. Some are questionable but not quite as far out. And a few seem to have at least a little real viability. We'll consider them in that order of acceptability.[3]

ON THE FRINGES

Crystal healing, which got its start in contemporary America in California (no surprise there), involves placing crystals of quartz and other colorful minerals on various parts of the body. Healthful energy is supposed to pass through the rocks, release tension, and tune up the body's vibrations.

Throughout history, in many different parts of the world, objects called talismans or amulets have been thought to possess magical powers useful in healing. Often these powers have supposedly come from indwelling spirits. The New Age use of crystals in a similar manner is just the latest version of this ancient occult idea. Needless to say, the practice is completely lacking in scientific validation.

Reflexology, which traces its roots to ancient China, is a form of body massage that tries to treat disease and keep the patient's "life force" in balance. That's a common theme in New Age therapies—that the life of each person is part of the universal "lifeforce," or "life energy," and that in order to promote true health, we have to learn how to manipulate this stream of energy.

The way this is supposed to work is that areas on the soles and sides of the feet, which reflexologists have all mapped out, govern "energy channels" that are spread throughout the body. When specific points on the foot are massaged, the practitioner can sense and unclog blocked channels. Working the big toe, for example, is supposed to relieve a headache. Massaging the left arch should help a bellyache. This practice also lacks scientific support.

Aromatherapy is another ancient Chinese invention, a form of herbal treatment. The idea here is that illnesses can be cured by massaging aromatic oils into the skin, like Ms. Jonas's use of rosemary on fibrous tissues in the breast. Sometimes the plant extracts are used as bath oils, they're inhaled, or in rare cases they're even ingested.

We know that certain scents do provoke strong reactions and that vanilla's aroma can be relaxing. But there is no solid evidence that scents cure diseases.

Ayur-Veda comes to us from ancient India. The books describing it were translated into English by the Maharishi Mahesh Yogi, who also brought us transcendental meditation a few decades ago. More recently, a couple of books preaching its virtues have been best-sellers in this country: *Quantum Healing: Exploring the Frontiers of Mind-Body Medicine* and *Perfect Health: The Complete Mind-Body Guide*. Both were written by Deepak Chopra, a doctor specializing in endocrinology.

The claim here is that all illnesses are caused by imbalances in bodily functions like breathing, circulation, and metabolism. Treatment involves meditation, massage, and herbal medicines. A twenty-minute drip of warm, herbal oil onto the forehead, for instance, is supposed to be good for insomnia, high blood pressure, and digestive troubles. Once again, evidence is lacking.

Homeopathy is a form of treatment growing out of the teachings of Samuel Hahnemann, a nineteenth-century German doctor. He said that symptoms of illness such as fever should not be suppressed. Rather, he administered natural drugs in tiny doses to produce the same symptoms. A feverish person, for example, would be given something to raise body temperature even further, since he believed the symptom indicated the body's effort to fight disease. Thus, more fever is therapeutic.

Some supportive studies have been reported in England, but they are far from conclusive, and this remains a definite fringe treatment with little acceptance from the medical establishment.

Herbalism is another ancient practice using medicines made from leaves, stems, seeds, and roots. These are rubbed on the body or consumed. Supporters claim these medications are as effective as manufactured drugs, but are often safer because they're natural.

Plant extracts are indeed the basis of many important medicines, and research is ongoing. A few herbs seem to have medicinal benefits. However, many herbal treatments are of questionable value at best, and in some cases they are known to make matters worse instead of improving one's health.

Naturopathy is another therapy from nineteenth-century Germany. It relies on such natural remedies as air, water, heat, massage, sunshine, and herbs to heal both mind and body. Adherents claim that illnesses can be cured by purging the body of poisons. To do that, saltwater baths, relaxation exercises, special breathing techniques, and fasting are used. It's possible that some of its remedies could be helpful, since many legitimate, tested drugs come from natural sources. But on the whole, this is another unproved method, as are all the rest in this section. The few controlled studies that have been done have failed to provide definitive conclusions.

Macrobiotics is yet another Chinese import. More than just a therapy for a specific illness (although it's best known as a cancer treatment), it's an ongoing dietary and health discipline stressing vegetarianism. The goal is to achieve optimal health by balancing yin (passive energy) and yang (active energy) foods. Foods are classified not by their nutrient composition but according to "activity characteristics" of the universe as defined by oriental philosophy.

Rolfing is a form of deep, sometimes painful massage of the body's fascia—connective material that holds the muscles together like the skin on a sausage. The idea of founder Ida Rolf is that the body "remembers" physical and emotional traumas in the fascia, which bind and shorten when traumatized, causing the rest of the body to compensate and so become misaligned. Thus, the massage restores health by returning the fascia to their original lengths.

Shiatsu is another form of massage, this time coming from Japan and more than a thousand years old. It's a rhythmic, fairly deep massage using pressure points. Adherents claim it can both prevent and treat a variety of illnesses.

The Alexander technique focuses on the spine, viewing good posture as the key to health. To alleviate pain, therefore, practitioners teach patients how to achieve and maintain proper posture.

Color healing is one of the more bizarre New Age therapies. Practitioners simply shine colored light on the body to change its "aura" or "vibrations." Here again, the object is to get the body in tune with that "universal life force."

QUESTIONABLE THERAPIES

Guided imagery is presented as a way to enlist the mind in the healing of the body. Patients are helped to reach a state of deep relaxation, and then the practitioner or a recording "guides" them in visualizing their illness and wishing it away. They are told beforehand to study how their immune systems fight a particular ailment, and then in session they're led to imagine the antibodies and white blood cells killing the disease.

This technique has shown some promise in helping patients recover from minor surgery faster and with less pain. Some doctors also believe it helps with chronic pain, tumors, and long-lasting infections. As best we can tell, whatever benefits it offers come primarily from reducing stress in patients, which is no cure-all but no small thing, either.

Chiropractic is a practice that has already gained wide acceptance in the United States. A chiropractor is a doctor with advanced training, but he/she is not a medical doctor. Most medical doctors are still wary of chiropractic, especially when advocates claim that because almost every nerve in the body runs through the spinal cord, they can treat all kinds of physical problems just by "adjusting" the vertebrae. There is only anecdotal testimony—no scientific evidence—to support such claims.

But studies have shown that chiropractic manipulations of the spine can relieve neck and lower back pain, and a few hospitals have chiropractors on staff for that specific purpose. Chiropractic manipulation restricted to spinal disorders has some viability, but when expanded to include disorders, chiropractic should be viewed with skepticism. When other neurological problems and symptoms are not relieved by manipulation, the chiropractor should refer the patient to a medical specialist, such as a neurologist, orthopedist, or a neurosurgeon.

TREATMENTS WITH SOME VIABILITY

Biofeedback is a technique that has proven useful in preventing or alleviating migraine or tension headaches, mild high blood pressure, chronic pain, stress and anxiety disorders, and incontinence. Before it's used, however, physical causes of the problems must be ruled out, and it normally is used in conjunction with other treatments.

Patients are attached painlessly to sensors that monitor temperature, blood pressure, blood flow, and sweat. They then watch a monitor displaying their readings or listen to a tone that reveals how close they're getting to the desired result, be it muscle relaxation, a lowered heart rate, warming of the hands, or whatever. The patients consciously try to influence their bodily system to the specific goal.

We don't know why some autonomic bodily functions can be controlled to a certain extent just by concentrating on them through the use of biofeedback devices. What we do know is that it seems to work and that it's gaining wider acceptance all the time, even being offered at such a prestigious place as the Mayo Clinic. Many insurers will now pay for training sessions as well.

Realize, however, that no one can exercise perfect control over autonomic functions or make the method work every time without fail. We cannot fully control all our autonomic functions any more than we can control outward circumstances. Only God, who created our bodies, can bring full restoration to wounded bodies and broken spirits.

Hypnosis is another apparently effective therapy whose way of helping we don't understand. What we do know is that studies show that about 94 percent of patients who try it get some benefit, if nothing more than relaxation.[4] It was accepted as a legitimate treatment by the American Medical Association (AMA) more than thirty-five years ago.

Some of the ways hypnosis seems to help include the following: asthmatics are able to breathe easier; Parkinson's disease victims are relieved of their tremors; ulcer patients seem able to control the release of stomach acid; burn patients recover quicker and with less medication; smokers are able to kick the habit; diabetic children are better able to follow their diet, exercise, and drug programs. Hypnosis doesn't cure anything by itself, but it does appear to help the healing process.

How does it work? Patients are helped to relax deeply by focusing on an object, a voice, or a mental image. As best we can tell, this stimulates the limbic system, the control center in the brain for emotion and many involuntary bodily functions. Brain-wave patterns change, pulse and respiration slow, and blood pressure falls. Then the limbic system responds to suggestions from the therapist to lower the output of stomach acid, open blood vessels, or whatever is appropriate to the illness being treated.

Hypnosis works best with people who are motivated and easily hypnotized, which leads some researchers to think it primarily has a placebo effect: those hypnotized believe and so receive benefits from the procedure.

Clearly, hypnosis cannot be used to make patients act in violation of their moral beliefs, no matter how many movies about evil "mind benders" suggest otherwise. But however it works, hypnosis certainly can help many patients.

Having stated the case for hypnosis, however, we also have to issue a strong caution and conclude that on balance, it is best avoided. Why? Primarily because it opens patients to outside influence in all three parts of the person. People under hypnosis surrender control of themselves. Becoming passive, they make themselves extremely vulnerable to harmful influence, even when the therapist is legitimate.

Second, while some studies indicate that hypnosis has therapeutic value, as we've said, many questions remain unanswered about what it really does and how. So even though it is an AMA-approved treatment, hypnosis still is considered a fringe kind of treatment by most medical professionals.

Acupuncture is one of the alternative treatments you've probably heard the most about. It's another Chinese import, almost three thousand years old, and it involves inserting fine needles into the body at specific points, primarily to ease pain. (A related therapy is *acupressure,* which uses fingers rather than needles.) It has been found to work well in relieving chronic back pain and the pain of arthritis and rheumatism. Some practitioners also report success in treating bronchial asthma, and others have found it helpful in relieving the chronic pain of premenstrual syndrome and spastic colon.

A study at Lincoln Hospital in New York found that acupuncture had a 60 percent success rate in keeping hard-core drug addicts straight for three months,[5] which is better than most other drug treatment programs manage. Studies, however, may be misleading, as many of them lack sound scientific methods.

Those who use acupuncture believe the body has defined pathways of energy running throughout it. Pain or sickness results when that energy flow is disrupted. Points on the skin along those pathways are related to specific organs and bodily functions, and stimulating them with the needles or, sometimes, heat somehow puts that energy flow back into balance. The best scientific explanation is that the heat or needles somehow stimulate the brain to release endorphins, chemicals that block pain.

In about half the states, acupuncture can only be performed by a medical doctor. At the time of this writing, twenty-one states license nondoctor practitioners. But it remains an inexact therapy; much depends on the individual skill and habits of the practitioner. Remember, too, that acupuncture is based on Eastern spiritual beliefs that are far closer to the New Age idea of our "oneness with the universe" than they are to a biblical understanding of God's orderly, nonmystical creation of our physical bodies. Proponents like to refer to mystical auras emanating from our bodies and talk about tapping into our "energy channels." All this ignores and even dismisses God the Creator. This makes acupuncture extremely suspect under any circumstance.

WHAT TO DO?

As the name "alternative therapies" suggests, the methods we have described, even those that appear to have at least some validity, should be secondary to conventional, scientific medicine. There is no substitute for a well-trained, competent doctor who knows you and has earned your trust. Only in consultation with your physician, after standard remedies have been considered, should you even think about other approaches.

Some of the fringe treatments are clearly without foundation and should never be used. Yet people do use them, people who are either ignorant or desperate, because they provide a false hope for a level of health or longevity that simply may not be possible.

One good thing we can see again from the relative success of certain therapies like biofeedback and hypnotism is that the mind and body are intimately connected. We have been making that point throughout this book; they serve to confirm it.

What about the value of physical exercise? There's a lot of talk, equipment, and programs dealing with it these days, and the implication is sometimes given that it will add years and years to your life, with all the energy of a teenager until the day you die. That's a bit of hyperbole, but there is a sense in which we're given false hopes about what exercise can do for us. We need to be as realistic about exercise as we are about what any form of therapy can do for us.

Having said that, however, we're firm believers in physical fitness. As we said in chapter 3, and as we'll develop in more detail in chapters 8 and 9, having things like our weight, blood pressure, and cholesterol level under control can lengthen our lives and add to their quality for as long as we're on this earth. It's no panacea for all that ails us, but it definitely helps. We remember when James Dobson, our friend and a noted author, suffered a heart attack a few years ago. His doctors told him afterward that his regular exercise, mostly in the form of playing basketball several times each week, had strengthened his heart and made the attack much less severe than it would have been otherwise.

We've seen now the major forms of physical (and to some extent mental) treatment that are increasingly popular but that give people, for the most part, only fruitless hopes for health and longevity. Many of them are related to what's called the New Age movement. That movement's spokespeople say a lot about whole-person health, and like us they include the spiritual and mental parts of the individual in their definition and discussion.

Therefore, to understand what New Agers have in mind for us, and to distinguish their ideas of whole-person health from our own, we turn our attention to their teachings in the next chapter.

TO YOUR HEALTH

1. Why are people drawn to New Age forms of therapy?

2. What spiritual dangers, if any, might there be in submitting to a New Age treatment?

3. If you had lower back pain and your doctor said surgery was the only solution, would you be willing to give chiropractic a try first? Why or why not? How about acupuncture? Why or why not?

4. Do you know anyone who actually tried an alternative treatment? If so, what was the outcome?

7

AN OLD NEW AGE DECEIT

Mrs. Green was concerned about her daughter Jane. Jane had become involved with a New Age group that practiced astral projection (out-of-body experiences). The mother said, "When my daughter and I talk, if any disagreement comes up, she withdraws and says, 'Mother, you can't hurt me because I am really not here. I have left my body, and I am on the ceiling, looking down on us.' "

The above story, told by Karen Hoyt in her book *The New Age Rage*,[1] illustrates one of the psychological defense mechanisms sometimes developed by hurting people in the New Age movement. Clearly, it's not a healthy defense; Jane isn't facing her pain, and she isn't resolving anything. She's only avoiding reality for a time.

We might call Jane's defense bizarre, even psychotic. But she's only one of many who are caught up in the strange world of the New Age. Proponents of the movement talk a lot about whole-person health, and we looked at some of their physical therapies in the last chapter. Now we want to examine their perspective on the subject and see how it compares to the Christian understanding we're trying to provide. What we will find is that their heresies have been around for a very long time;

they've just been slickly packaged for the Western world. They're just old wolves in sheep's clothing.

THE BEATLES AND SHIRLEY MACLAINE

Just how big is this New Age movement? It's hard to say with confidence, because it's not an organized program with membership lists and a central leadership. The answer also depends on how you define the movement, on whether you include only hardcore adherents or add in people who might only agree with some of the movement's philosophies.

By the broader definition, however, the New Age has a lot of followers. For example, in a 1987 survey, 23 percent of Americans said they believe in reincarnation, one of the movement's best-known beliefs. The same percentage said they believe in astrology—that the future can be predicted from the position of the stars and planets. That's also a part of New Age thinking. And 25 percent said they believe in a nonpersonal energy or life force, which is yet another key principle.[2] Since the population of the United States is now about 250 million, we're talking about tens of millions of people who are at least open to the movement's teaching. And the number is increasing.

Although the New Age teachings are very old (more on that shortly), the rapid growth of the movement in this country really started with the hippie generation and its rebellion against traditional morals, its search for inner enlightenment aided by drugs, and its yearning for world peace and opposition to the Vietnam War. Popularizers like the Beatles came back from trips to Asia and told of gurus who had all the answers. Meditation techniques like yoga and transcendental meditation were introduced as ways to tap our hidden inner resources of wisdom and energy.

Though its roots on a popular level lie clearly in the sixties, the person who most brought attention to the movement was the actress Shirley MacLaine, through her books and the TV miniseries "Out on a Limb." That program, spread over five hours on two nights, captured the public's attention and got people talking and thinking. In it, Americans saw reincarnation, auras, out-of-body and near-death experiences, telepathy, candle meditation, extraterrestrial revelation and guidance, and spirit channeling.

Robert Burrows of the Spiritual Counterfeits Project said of MacLaine's series, "If she communicated anything, it was that all of these seemingly disparate things point to a single conclusion: Humanity is divine and immortal."[3] That message, not surprisingly, appeals to a lot of people.

NEW AGE ROOTS

We've mentioned a number of New Age ideas now, and they're probably sounding strange. But before we look at them more closely, we'd like to consider where they come from. What are the roots of the movement?

New Age thinking grows primarily out of Eastern religions, especially Zen Buddhism. Buddhism itself was founded by Siddhartha Gautama, called the Buddha, in the sixth and fifth centuries B.C. The Zen form dates from the fifth century A.D. So as you can see, this is indeed an ancient religion, even predating Christianity.

Some of the most prominent names in the movement— for example, Maharishi Mahesh Yogi, Guru Maharaj Ji, and Ram Dass—come straight from Buddhism. However, when Maharishi Mahesh Yogi introduced transcendental meditation to this country, he tried to hide its religious nature and play it up as a scientifically valid way to reduce stress.

Other proponents weren't so subtle. They preached Buddhism's critique of Western workaholism and materialism—of desire of any kind—themes that appealed to the young adults of the sixties, and they taught that through meditation and enlightenment we can all become little gods. Especially to people who feel powerless or as if life is out of control, that message continues to have great appeal.

Hinduism from India, founded in about 1500 B.C., also figures into the New Age movement. Individual gurus gained followings in the West, and many young people went to India to learn it there. Hinduism has numerous sects devoted to individual gods, but all the gods are seen as parts, or "aspects," of the one divine principle.

Native-American religion became a part of the mix as well, with its emphasis on things like the oneness of nature, spirit guides, and places of power. The great popularizer in this case was author Carlos Castaneda and his 1968 book *The Teachings of Don Juan: A Yaqui Way of Knowledge*. His fascinating stories of shamanism and its rites, including the use of peyote (a hallucinatory drug), attracted still more followers to the New Age.

Neopaganism, the worship of mother earth, is another part of the New Age that's growing on the fringes of the modern ecology movement. Each year on Earth Day, we can look forward to news reports about people who were out in meadows or on mountainsides, holding hands in a circle and worshiping the earth.

Yet another root of the New Age, one not so obviously religious in nature, is the humanistic psychology of such writer-practitioners as Abraham Maslow, Carl Rogers, and Rollo May. The message here is that people are basically good, that human potential is enormous, and that personal growth toward "self-actualization" is the highest goal. The self-actualized person at the top of Maslow's famous hierarchy of needs corresponds to the enlightened person in the world of Zen.

There are many smaller roots that feed into the New Age movement as well, and most of them are also ancient. Astrology, for instance, dates back to the Chaldeans and Assyrians, centuries before the time of Christ. Worship of female deities, which can now be found on the far fringes of the feminist movement, goes back thousands of years, too—it was part of the paganism God told the Israelites to destroy when they conquered Canaan.

Regarding these many ancient roots of the movement, Robert Burrows concluded, "The New Age movement is with us to stay. It is the wave of the future, because it has always been the way of the world."[4]

TEACHINGS OF THE NEW AGE

Where does the term "New Age" come from? Proponents of the movement believe humanity is currently between two ages. The old age we're leaving behind was marked by mankind's fall into ignorance. The emphasis was on reason and logic, which prevented us from recognizing the essential unity of everything. That, in turn, has caused all the ills in the world.

Gradually, however, more and more people are becoming enlightened, enough so that we're now on the verge of an epochal move forward. Humanity will emerge into a New Age, the culmination of history, as a new creature not bound by old conventions or ways of thinking but fully aware of and in tune with reality's unity. This is our great hope for a better tomorrow.

With so many religions and philosophies contributing to the New Age, we might wonder how it can be called a movement. There must be some common core of beliefs that ties it together, and indeed there is.

The central tenet of the New Age is called monism, the belief that everything in the universe is one substance, a vast, impersonal unity. New Agers call it "the one," "Universal Consciousness," and "Life Energy," among other things. Some might even call it "God" to accommodate the simple-minded. All people—and all cats, rats, rocks, socks, cars, and stars, for that matter—are a part of this unity. It doesn't appear that way to us in the materialistic West, of course, so we need to disconnect our rational minds and experience this unity in an altered state of consciousness. We need to be enlightened to perceive the true reality, the proponents argue.

The energy that makes up everything we see, including our bodies, is connected to this life energy, which is why the movement's physical therapies focus on manipulating the invisible flow of energy in the body. So whole-person health in the physical sense means getting your body in tune with the cosmic energy flow.

Healing help might also be had from people who have already reached a higher state of enlightenment and so are in contact with realities that go beyond the five senses. These include the psychic surgeons of South America and native American shamans.

Now here's a major step in the logical extension of monism's basic belief: Since all is one and we're a part of that oneness, that makes us the same as the one, or God. In other words, we're all gods, perfect spiritual beings, but most of us just don't know it yet. And our most basic need as human beings, therefore, is not a Savior to redeem us from our sins, but enlightenment so we can realize we're already divine.

Further, since we're divine, we have infinite potential, and we inherently possess all the power and wisdom of the universe. What's more, since all is really one, the things we see that "seem" to be distinct—all the objects in the material world—are actually illusory.

Another important, related belief is that since we are gods, we have no limits. Death, therefore, cannot be the end of anything, just a final stage of growth. It takes place within the illusory world, so it, too, is an illusion. The reality is that as part of the divine, changeless one, we are immortal.

From this perspective, if you accept it, reincarnation actually starts to make sense. After all, if everything in the universe is part of the same impersonal life force, we could be incarnated as anything. A tree, a pig, or a snail is every bit as much connected to this unity as a human being.

WHAT IT ALL MEANS

Obviously, the preceding discussion was a greatly condensed version of what New Agers believe. But it gives us enough of a feel for their essential teachings that we can hold them up for comparison with the truth revealed in the Bible.

In the physical health area, New Agers have a point when they emphasize the connectedness of all three parts of a person. Wholeness is an ongoing process of health, not just going to a doctor for a pill or an operation when a specific illness arises. As we saw in the previous chapter, however, many of their therapies are based on their dubious understanding of our nature and our connection to the life energy. It's downright dangerous, for example, to have a New Age practitioner of reflexology massaging the arch of your left foot to "unclog your energy channels" and thus relieve your bellyache when the real problem is an ulcer.

The Bible does not speak of an impersonal unity of which everything is a part. Rather, from the very beginning of the book of Genesis, it tells of an eternal, Creator God who spoke the universe and everything in it into being. We are not part of a divine whole but creatures made from the dust of the earth. The material world, including our bodies, is not an illusion, and healing does not come through an enlightenment reached in an altered state of consciousness.

In the spiritual and mental realm, our problem is not a lack of appreciation for our oneness with the universe but estrangement from God because of our sin. "For all have sinned and fall short of the glory of God" (Romans 3:23), the apostle Paul writes. The Bible also indicates, "For the wages of sin is death, but the gift of God is eternal life in Christ Jesus our Lord" (Romans 6:23).

Our sin not only separates us from God, but it also accounts for a lot of the pain in this world. Intentionally or otherwise, people inflict a lot of suffering on each other—parents on their children, spouses on spouses, friends on friends, and so on. And when a person is hurting from, say, abuse endured as a child at the hands of loved ones, feeling at one with the cosmos is not the answer. That person needs to learn to forgive (see, for example, Matthew 18:21-22); to know he or she is incredibly, unconditionally loved (Romans 5:8; 1 John 4:7-10); and to believe God somehow works everything out for good (Romans 8:28). He also will find emotional and spiritual comfort knowing that his loving Lord will never desert him (Hebrews 13:5).

Furthermore, some of the ways New Agers tap into the unseen world for guidance and prophecy—shamans, spirit channeling, and the like—are clearly condemned in the Bible: "Let no one be found among you . . . who practices divination or sorcery, interprets omens, engages in witchcraft, or casts spells, or who is a medium or spiritist or who consults the dead. Anyone who does these things is detestable to the Lord" (Deuteronomy 18:10-12).

As for our ultimate hope of immortality, it's not found in a New Age populated by people who have discovered they were divine all along. Death is real, and so is God's judgment on sin. "Just as man is destined to die once, and after that to face judgment" (Hebrews 9:27). Instead, hope comes from being reconciled to the Creator God through faith in Jesus Christ: "For God so loved the world that he gave his one and only Son, that whoever believes in him shall not perish but have eternal life" (John 3:16).

Scripture makes it plain that every person's destiny hinges on what is made of Jesus: "Anyone who does not believe God has made him out to be a liar, because he has not believed the testimony God has given about his Son. And this is the testimony: God has given us eternal life, and this life is in his Son. He who has the Son has life; he who does not have the Son of God does not have life" (1 John 5:10-12). Since Jesus is the only way to peace with God (see also John 14:6), we can't possibly enjoy full spiritual and mental health until we have committed our lives to Him.

DARKENED MINDS AVOID PAIN

Clearly, the New Age vision of humanity, of creation, and of what it means to be a whole and healthy person is at odds with the biblical perspective. Only one view can be right. So why is the New Age movement growing so rapidly?

As we've noted several times now, the natural but unhealthy human tendency is to avoid pain. And people whose minds are darkened (see Romans 1:18-32) yet who want peace and love and fulfillment are drawn to a philosophy that offers what they desire without the pain of the gospel. They will take the comfortable lie over the hard truth.

That was certainly the case with Jane, the young woman mentioned in the opening of this chapter. When her mother criticized her, Jane could pretend she was away. "I am not really here. I have left my body" she declared, and eventually she believed her grand delusion, which was merely a comforting lie.

It's tough for proud people to admit they are sinners, to agree that they're hopeless on their own, to submit to a God who says that to love Him is to obey His commands (see 1 John 2:3-6). It's much easier to embrace a movement that says you're divine already, not limited to one mortal body. *I have unlimited potential and just need to tap into it*, one can argue, buying the lie that immortality is a given.

As we've seen, the roots of the New Age movement are ancient. People have been buying into those same lies for thousands of years—they really are old wolves in sheep's clothing. And they're devouring millions of unsuspecting sheep today. So the bad news is that the New Age is a fraud, but the good news is that true whole-person health can be ours when we face the truth about ourselves and the God who made us, and do things His way.

At this point, we've seen a number of things that go wrong in the quest for true, lasting health. But now, in the third part of this book, we turn to the good news of how we can develop and maintain such health. We begin by looking in the next chapter at how you, no matter what your condition in any of the three areas of your person, can start to grow healthy today.

To Your Health

1. In your own words, what is monism?

2. How does New Age philosophy view God?

3. How would you explain the gospel to a New Age believer?

4. How does the New Age prophecy about the future compare to what you know of biblical prophecy?

Part 3

The Road to Whole-Person Health

8

MOVING FROM SICKNESS TO HEALTH

Karen came to us as a patient after having already been to
several Christian therapists. They hadn't been able to help
her much for one reason or another. We soon recognized
that Karen had multiple personality disorder (MPD). She had
actually developed several distinct personalities, and she
would move back and forth between them.

Like most people afflicted with MPD, Karen had been a
victim of childhood sexual abuse. She was carrying such tremendous unresolved pain that she had split into different
personalities in order to avoid those pockets of terrifying experience. The other "people" inside her didn't share Karen's past,
so they didn't have to feel her pain.

Fortunately for Karen, we had on our staff a therapist who
is like a female Dr. Marcus Welby. Tender yet firm, and a good
listener, our Dr. Welby would spend hour upon hour with a patient like Karen, as if she were her only patient. This doctor took
Karen in, listened to her, let her cry, and helped her to discover
and discuss the awful pain in her past that had led to her disorder. In addition, our Madam Dr. Welby gradually, over a fairly
long period of time, helped Karen gain a sense of self-worth.
She also involved Karen with a Christian ministry, where Karen

began to focus on the needs of others, have the joy of accomplishment, and feel God's blessing.

Eventually, we're happy to report, Karen's personality did reintegrate. The multiple personalities faded away, and the true, healthy Karen emerged.

Another patient, Tom, was a seminary student. He was psychotic, which means his mind had broken away from reality. In fact, when we put him in the hospital, he went on rounds like a member of the staff, telling people he was Dr. Minirth!

Tom did have enough realistic insight, however, to understand that everyone has problems, that he had a problem, and that it's OK to get help. We began by giving him an antipsychotic medication. We told him he needed to face and deal with the pain inside that he was trying to avoid, which Tom chose to do. And we helped him develop, again over a period of time, a true and strong sense of self-worth based on the love and provision of God in Christ Jesus.

Because of Tom's decision to face his pain and the help we were able to give him, he recovered from his psychosis and went on to finish seminary and become a pastor. The last we heard, he has a thriving ministry in a church in one of the western states.

Getting Healthy Is a Process

Of course, few of us use such extreme ways of avoiding pain or conflict as Karen and Tom did. More likely, we use one of the common defense mechanisms listed in chapter 5. Nonetheless, the stories of Karen and Tom illustrate a number of the points we want to make as we discuss how you can move from sickness to health. No matter where you are on a scale of health (perhaps as measured by the self-test in chapter 3), you can have the kind of whole-person health every person wants to enjoy.

The first thing that needs to be said is that *getting healthy is a process*, one that takes some time. Whatever condition you're in now—physically, mentally/emotionally, and spiritually—it has taken you a number of years to get there. Your fitness (or lack thereof) is the result of many attitudes and habits applied over however many years you've been making your own decisions about your lifestyle.

Consequently, it only stands to reason—and experience verifies—that moving from where you are now to where you want to be is also going to take time. You'll need to develop some new disciplines and establish some new habits. For most of us, that's a struggle, and we will falter a few times (or maybe a lot) along the way. We need to expect that making healthy changes will take time, and so *we need to be patient with ourselves*. As simple as it sounds, that's a vital truth.

Karen's progression toward mental and emotional health, as well as spiritual health, took time. That loving therapist invested hours and hours with her. Karen herself spent many more hours in prayer, in study, and in service to others. All this transpired over a period of years. Tom's recovery was likewise a gradual process. The decision to face his pain was only the first step on his road to recovery. And that's just the way we would expect it to be. We believe God still does miracles of instant healing, but we also believe they are the rare exception rather than the rule. So once again, as we begin to work at improving our health, we need to remember that it's a process and to be patient and persistent.

MENTAL AND SPIRITUAL HEALTH

The same major prescriptions apply to developing both mental and spiritual health, so we'll look at them together. This is another illustration of how closely connected our different parts are. For example, one of the keys to either kind of health is to learn to accept pain as a part of life.

In chapter 4, we quoted psychiatrist and best-selling author Scott Peck as saying most people don't recognize or acknowledge that life is full of difficulty. They try to avoid its pain rather than learn and grow through it. Peck adds, "This tendency to avoid problems and the emotional suffering inherent in them is the primary basis of all human mental illness. Since most of us have this tendency to a greater or lesser degree, most of us are mentally ill to a greater or lesser degree, lacking complete mental health."[1]

ACCEPT THE PAIN

We concur, which is why we say that the road to good health has to include a growing acceptance of pain's presence in our lives. That doesn't mean we like pain or take a fatalistic attitude toward suffering, but it does mean we accept it as a part of life, we face it and deal with it rather than trying to avoid it, and we look for the good that can come out of it. (For a helpful treatment of the value to be found in suffering, see *Gold in the Making*, by Ron Lee Davis.) Karen and Mike both came to this understanding, and it was crucial to their recovery from serious mental illness.

The spiritual side of this issue is that if we don't accept pain as a part of life, we can grow very bitter toward the God who we think should not be allowing it into our lives. We can also come to doubt His love for us, which in turn can kill our interest in reading and studying His Word and in praying to Him. When this happens, we may move away from God, which means a sure decline in spiritual health, not improvement.

Shirley, the young woman with sarcoidosis (chapter 3), could easily have felt abandoned by God and so could abandon Him in turn. Her chronic pain was hard to understand and accept. But she chose to trust Him instead, to believe He knew what He was doing in allowing such pain to be part of her life, and to hope that somehow He would bring something good out of it. She spent a lot of time in Bible study and prayer. And as a result of all these things, she now is one of the healthiest people, mentally and spiritually, that we've known.

Depression is a good example of a kind of pain that can actually be beneficial to us. Some depressions are endogenous, meaning they arise from a chemical imbalance in the body, and so they need a chemical treatment. But many depressions result from some loss in our lives, like the death of a loved one.

When that's the case, the depression is a normal, healthy, God-given response to the triggering event. It's a symptom that something is wrong and needs attention—in this case, that we've suffered a significant loss and need to slow down and take the time to grieve.

Unfortunately, many Christians believe they should never be depressed, that it's somehow sinful or at least spiritually immature. They think their faith should make them immune to such pain. They are thus avoiding it, not facing it, and so by Peck's definition are "lacking complete mental [and, we might add, spiritual] health."

SEE LIFE FROM GOD'S PERSPECTIVE

A second key to mental and spiritual health, consistent with the first, is to gradually learn to see our lives from God's perspective. As we do, we gain a whole new outlook on things and a much higher level of health. We are able to recognize the ultimate lie of Satan, that meaning to our lives comes by protecting ourselves, improving our position, and acquiring possessions. We learn the ultimate truth, that lasting security and significance and satisfaction come from submitting our lives to Christ, letting Him be our Lord (see Figure 6).

We know one married couple, for example, who at the time of this writing have been separated by one thousand miles, against their will, for several months. He made a job transfer, and she's still back in their old house, trying to get it sold. From a human perspective, their situation is a frustrating dilemma. From a simple Christian perspective, it's hard to understand why a loving God would allow two marriage partners to be separated and a father to be apart from his son.

This husband and wife certainly don't claim to have God's perspective on the matter all figured out. But they do know that because of the separation, they've developed a deeper appreciation for each other than they ever had before. They pray for each other more consistently. They're learning a greater lesson about being patient and waiting on the Lord than they had ever learned before.

Figure 6
THE ULTIMATE LIE AND THE ULTIMATE TRUTH

THE ULTIMATE LIE

The ultimate lie of Satan is that security, significance, and satisfaction result from:

1. Protecting the person
2. Improving one's position
3. Acquiring possessions

THE ULTIMATE TRUTH

True security, significance, and satisfaction result from:

1. Submitting my person
2. Yielding my position
3. Giving my possessions to the rule of Christ.

An intimate, personal relationship with Christ is the only way to true security, significance, and satisfaction.

Now think about their situation. Will their house sell and their family be reunited? Yes, and it will probably have happened by the time you read this book. Before long, the pain of the present trial will be forgotten. But the things they've gained through the experience will remain. From God's perspective, in the light of eternity and His goal of seeing all Christians become ever more like Jesus, will what they've gone through have been worth it? We believe so. And the more they gain and then hold on to that perspective, the healthier they'll be.

Archibald Hart, a noted Christian psychologist, writes about developing this way of seeing things in the context of overcoming the depression associated with loss: "You must pull back and *put the loss in some larger perspective*, so the loss does not continue to dominate your whole life. As Christians, we must begin to see the loss from God's perspective. We begin to see how insignificant some of the things we grieve over are when put into the context of the larger scheme of things."[2]

In saying that, Dr. Hart was echoing the apostle Paul when he wrote, "Therefore we do not lose heart. Though outwardly we are wasting away, yet inwardly we are being renewed day by day. For our light and momentary troubles are achieving for us an eternal glory that far outweighs them all. So we fix our eyes not on what is seen, but on what is unseen. For what is seen is temporary, but what is unseen is eternal" (2 Corinthians 4:16-18).

Those verses could summarize this entire book. Living with the pressures and demands of everyday life, it's easy to get wrapped up in an earthbound perspective. But there's an even greater reality that can give us strength and is, in fact, essential to a healthy mind and spirit, and we must never allow ourselves to lose sight of it.

That perspective can truly be life changing. The deeper and more intense our pain, however, the harder it may be to be open to that point of view, and the longer it may take. Sometimes the answer to "Why?" is a long time coming, and sometimes we never find it in this lifetime (as happened to the men of faith described in Hebrews 11 [note verse 39]). So once again, we need to be patient with ourselves, and we need to trust God. That sounds simple for us to say, but we know that for many people it's a very tough choice to make. Like Karen, Mike, and Shirley, however, we *must* make it if we're ever to grow.

HAVE A BRAIN TRANSPLANT

Just how do we gain a greater understanding of God's perspective? That question leads us to the third key to increasing mental and spiritual health. It involves what the Bible calls a brain transplant. Actually, the apostle Paul puts it this way: "Do not conform any longer to the pattern of this world, but be transformed by the renewing of your mind. Then you will be able to test and approve what God's will is—his good, pleasing and perfect will" (Romans 12:2).

To become spiritually and mentally more healthy, we need to be transformed by developing renewed minds. And that happens primarily as we fill our minds with God's Word through reading, study, memorization, and meditation. These are all things that Christians know they "ought" to do, and our general failure to do them consistently may be somewhat guilt-inducing as we bring up the subject here. In addition, memorizing Bible verses may sound like "kid stuff" to some readers, and meditation may make you think only of the kind of New Age practice we discussed in the last chapter.

We hope, however, that you can appreciate the importance of growing steadily in seeing life from God's perspective. And if you do, then filling our minds with His revealed Word is obviously the most logical and best way to do it. The Bible itself expresses this more poetically. David the psalmist said, "Blessed is the man . . . [whose] delight is in the law of the Lord, and on his law he meditates day and night. He is like a tree planted by streams of water, which yields its fruit in season and whose leaf does not wither. Whatever he does prospers" (Psalm 1:1-3). Job, even in the midst of his suffering and the false accusations of his "friends," said, "I have treasured the words of [God's] mouth more than my daily bread" (Job 23:12).

In Psalm 119, a grand tribute to God's Word, the psalmist wrote, "Oh, how I love your law! I meditate on it all day long. Your word is a lamp to my feet and a light for my path" (vv. 97, 105). In other words, knowing God's Word, the Bible, is a practical way to gain His perspective on life and so make wise decisions.

We relate this back to what people like Karen and Tom have gone through, and to Hart's recommendation that we place our losses in proper context. So much of the personal loss that causes us pain, so much of the anger we feel toward God, others, and ourselves, and so much of the anxiety we feel about possible future losses arises from our human concern about our person, position, and possessions. In terms of our person, we've been rejected, or we fear we might lose the love of some significant person. In terms of position, we've been humiliated, or we know we've done something wrong—perhaps we harbor a secret bad habit—and we fear what discovery would do to our reputation. In terms of possession, we have been through hard times financially, and we fear the loss of a job.

The Bible offers all of us what we all desperately need: the assurance that in Christ, no matter what happens, our person and position are secure, and the possessions we need will be provided. In the case of both Karen and Tom, we wrote of how they needed to develop a sense of healthy self-worth. And where does that come from? Only from believing—based on passages like John 3:16, Romans 5:8, Psalm 103, and Hebrews 4:14-16—that the holy God of the universe knows us in all our weakness, loves us with an unchanging love, made it possible through Christ for us to know Him and fellowship with Him forever, and welcomes us with open arms. When we are solidly grounded in those truths, we have the strongest possible foundation on which spiritual and mental health can be built.

SEEK HELP FROM OTHERS

Karen and Tom's stories, and Shirley's too, also point to a fourth key to health. Namely, they sought appropriate help from others, without which they probably would not have recovered from their mental illnesses. Even "normal" people get into bad habits; they get lazy about doing the things that promote health; and they have a hard time seeing themselves objectively. So we all need someone, be it a spouse, friend, counselor, or Bible study partner, who knows what's going on in our lives and can give us helpful feedback.

Let's say, for example, that in light of the value of renewing your mind with Scripture, you decide to read your Bible every day and memorize two verses each week. You start out with the best of intentions, and maybe you stick to that schedule for the first week or two. But then you become very busy, you go through a stressful time, you go on vacation, or you catch a cold—something happens to disrupt your routine, and you haven't yet made a habit of your time with the Bible. Before you know it, you realize like Suzy Morgan in chapter 2 that it's been weeks if not months since you spent any time on your own in God's Word.

But now suppose that when you first decide to read and memorize, you mention it to a good friend over lunch. "That sounds like a good idea," your friend says. "I think I'll try the same thing."

"Why don't we talk on the phone every Friday night and compare how we're doing," you answer. "Maybe we can even recite our memory verses to each other. Knowing we're going to be talking about it will probably help me stick with it."

Your friend agrees, and you're off and running. And lo and behold, you find that the anticipation of that weekly phone call does exert a subtle pressure to meet your commitment. You just don't want to have to say you blew it in the last week. This is called *accountability*, and it's a tremendous help in getting us to do the things we need to do. It's the key to the success of such support groups as Alcoholics Anonymous and Weight Watchers.

LEARN TO RELAX

Key number five is to learn to relax, to pull back often from the frantic pace of modern life and be refreshed. Make time for family, for hobbies and recreation, and for friends. Several of the statements in "Your Health Profile" self-test (chapter 3) point to the need for time to get away, to calm down, to take a break from our normal work and other responsibilities.

This seems like such an obvious need, such a clear way to improve our health, yet it's usually not an "urgent" need, so it's easily forgotten in the busyness of our lives. Don't let that continue. Find the time. Write it into your schedule. Make it a priority.

Recently I (Randy) began to work twenty-four to forty-eight hour shifts at an emergency hospital. The extended time of seeing patients is followed by five days off. After an intense twenty-four-hour shift (I'm in residence all day and night, subject to call for any emergency), I have found that a short drive to the mountains and a swim in a cool stream with my family are both relaxing and invigorating. The adventure is fun for the entire family, including our cocker spaniel/retriever puppy, Lucky.

Your work schedule probably is less demanding, yet the need to relax and follow times of work with times of play is no less. Again, we tend to forget or dismiss our need to relax. We need to work at making time for play. Establish it as a priority.

CONSIDER PHYSICAL CAUSES

A sixth key to health is to realize that sometimes, what seems to you like a purely mental or emotional problem may in fact have a biochemical base. In telling Tom's story, we mentioned that antipsychotic drugs were a real help to him. We also said that some depressions are rooted in a chemical imbalance in the body. When there is a physical component to such a problem, a physical, medical treatment may well be in order.

Please understand that we're not saying you should try to diagnose yourself. And you certainly shouldn't try to medicate yourself. But we are saying that you should be aware of and open to the possibility that you may need medical care for your problem. Don't rule that out or think it's somehow unspiritual. If you have a serious or persistent problem, seek professional help from someone who will consider all the possibilities in diagnosing and treating your illness.

This perspective is foundational to the Minirth-Meier clinics. We have on staff medical doctors as well as counselors, and all our people know how to help patients draw on God's healing resources. So when patients come to us, we're able to look at and treat the whole person. We're convinced it's the best way to aid hurting people.

Obviously, we could fill entire books discussing how to develop mental and spiritual health. We have only scratched the surface here. But if you begin to apply the principles we've outlined, you will grow steadily more healthy. To measure your progress, retake the self-test in chapter 3 from time to time. It provides a simple yet good yardstick, and seeing your score climb will give you further motivation to keep doing the things that promote health. But remember, be patient with yourself.

PHYSICAL HEALTH

The whole person demonstrates a strong, healthy spirit and emotions. In contrast, when either spirit or emotions is weak, your physical health is threatened. Furthermore, when your emotions are drained and depression or anxiety dominates, you are vulnerable to a host of physical ills.

And the opposite is true: when physically you are drained, your emotions can deflate. A person working overtime six days a week for one month may have a great paycheck, but he also may develop an "I don't care" attitude. Fatigue has stolen his energy and drained his emotions. He is ready for depression and even physical ailments, such as insomnia, lightheadedness, and weight loss.

Physical health often seems the least important of our three elements. Yet life is more enjoyable, and it's much easier to be productive, when we're in good health. And the great majority of us could be in better shape than we are. Most important, with good health we are able to have a longer, more vibrant life for Christ.

For some of us, like Shirley, there are definite limits to what we can do physically, yet we can still have rich and fulfilling lives if we're healthy in the other areas. The self-test in chapter 3 is again a good place to begin our look at developing good physical health. The test highlights the areas of concern: weight, exercise, diet, sleep, blood pressure level, and so on. If you haven't already completed "Your Health Profile," do so now to get a general idea of the state of your condition.

Of course, immortality in the New Age sense is a myth, and eternal youth is also a vain hope. Nonetheless, we can do things to increase the quality and length of our lives. We can, in fact, reduce the risk of experiencing a deadly disease by more than 50 percent! Let us explain.

Seven major disease processes kill 1.6 million Americans annually, accounting for nearly 75 percent of the deaths from chronic disease. And we can reduce our risk of suffering from each of those seven "biggies" by the lifestyle choices we make. Those deadly diseases are coronary artery disease (that is, heart attack), cancer, stroke, emphysema, AIDS, diabetes, and cirrhosis (usually of the liver). Some of us are genetically predisposed to one or more of these illnesses, and there's nothing science can do for us yet in such cases. Most of us, however, can take measures to reduce our chances of getting them. Diet alone may prevent one-third of the annual 500,000 cancer deaths and may greatly diminish the number of deaths from heart attack, stroke, and diabetes as well.

The basics of a healthy, well-balanced diet were sketched in chapter 3, but let us add a little more detail here. Numerous studies have shown that daily consumption of fruits and vegetables is associated with a decreased risk of lung, prostate, bladder, esophagus, stomach, and colon cancers. Those food items contain essential nutrients, and they may also help prevent heart disease.

You've probably heard a lot in the last few years about dietary fiber. The term covers a variety of food components, abundant in fruits, vegetables, and whole grains, that are not digested by the body. Evidence indicates fiber helps to prevent colon cancer, and it indirectly reduces heart disease by binding with cholesterol (which comes from meat and dairy products) and other fats in the intestinal tract and preventing their absorption into the blood. Cutting down on fat in the diet can reduce the risk of heart disease and of colon, breast, and prostate cancers. It can also slow the loss of muscle fiber; the average person loses it at a rate of 2-5 percent every ten years. At this time, fat makes up 40 percent of the caloric intake of the average American. A more healthy figure would be about 25 percent.[3]

Smoked foods (for example, hams, sausages, and fish) absorb the tars that arise from incomplete burning in the smoking process. Those tars contain numerous carcinogens similar to those in tobacco smoke. Nitrites used in prepared meats and salt-cured and pickled foods may also increase the risk of cancer. Consumption of these foods should therefore be limited. Refined sugar should be used moderately as well, since excess sugar is turned into fat and may aggravate such common conditions as migraine headaches, hypoglycemia, diabetes, and premenstrual syndrome.

Salt may also contribute to migraines and premenstrual syndrome, as well as fluid retention. Most important, salt in excess of 4,000 milligrams daily has been shown to elevate blood pressure. For that reason, salt intake ought to be limited; avoid foods high in sodium. By the way, canned fruits and vegetables are much higher in sodium than frozen foods, and frozen foods are higher than fresh.

As for vitamin supplements, a well-balanced diet will supply all the nutrients needed for good health. However, there's no harm in taking a generic brand multivitamin if you so choose. But don't waste your money on costly "natural" vitamins from a health food store—vitamins are vitamins. The expensive ones are chemically identical to the generic ones.

Calcium is necessary to maintain strong bones and teeth, and it aids in numerous chemical reactions within the body, including proper muscle function. Women above age forty-five, especially if postmenopausal, should ingest 1,200 to 1,500 mg daily to prevent osteoporosis (thinning of the bones). That seems to suggest plenty of milk each day; after all, one eight-ounce glass of milk has 240 mg of calcium. To limit fat intake, however, the kind of milk is important. Skim milk is preferable to 2 percent milk, which is preferable to whole milk. The same reasoning applies to various cheeses. Note, however, that if you have a history of kidney stones, you'll need to limit your intake of calcium.

Besides diet, the keys to reducing the risk of those seven major illnesses include no tobacco of any kind, using alcohol moderately (1 oz. per day) or not at all, practicing monogamous sex with your spouse, getting adequate rest, and keeping your weight and cholesterol under control. We'll throw one more statistic at you regarding weight: A study by the American Cancer Society showed that obese women (40 percent above their ideal weight) had up to 55 percent greater mortality from cancer than women of normal weight, while obese men had up to 33 percent higher mortality from cancer than men of normal weight.[4]

Whenever you contemplate major lifestyle changes—a new diet or exercise program, for example—you should first consult your doctor. You may have heard that disclaimer so many times that it's easy to pass off, but a doctor's input into your plans can be vital to your health. You may discover, for instance, that certain kinds of food or exercise could do you more harm than good. So don't skip this step, especially if you haven't had a physical exam for several years or you're significantly overweight. Get your cholesterol and blood pressure checked, too, so you know just where you stand with those and what dietary changes may be in order.

In starting an exercise program, here are a few common-sense suggestions. First, consult your doctor before you do anything. Second, choose an activity you will enjoy and stay with. There are so many sports and exercise machines to select from these days that you should be able to find several you can enjoy and afford. Third, put some variety into your program so you don't become bored. If you like to walk but cover the same route every day, you will probably tire of it before long. Explore different paths. Ride a bike or swim once in a while instead of walking. Find a partner to exercise with you at least part of the time. Use a portable stereo if listening to music will make the time pass more enjoyably. (But be careful if you're outdoors that you don't block out the sound of approaching cars and kids on skateboards!)

Finally, start slowly, and build your endurance and speed gradually. The goal is a lifetime of basic fitness, not the Olympic team. Taking your time will avoid overtaxing your body and reduce the risk of injury. Do stretching exercises before and after a workout of any kind. And have fun!

Better health is possible for each of us, regardless of what kind of condition we're starting from. We all have room for improvement, and even the most out-of-shape in any area can make steady progress. But we have to start, we have to stay with it, and we need to be patient with ourselves.

In the next chapter we will look at how to maintain this whole-person health we are starting to develop. Some of our daily habits do us more harm than good, and some new habits can make a tremendous improvement in our lives. In fact, those new habits will go to the heart of whole-person health—ways to restore and then strengthen our body, mind, and spirit.

To Your Health

1. Are you usually patient with yourself, or do you tend to expect "overnight" results when you start doing something healthy? Why?

2. When we're in the midst of a painful situation, how can we keep from growing bitter toward God?

3. When we're depressed, how might we respond to others who think we should be able to get over it immediately?

4. With what current difficulty could you benefit from a clearer understanding of God's perspective?

9

STAYING HEALTHY

Fran, a Houston homemaker, came to us very depressed. The reason for her illness, she felt, was a lack of closeness between her and her husband. It was true that their communication tended to be superficial, and Fran wanted much more.

As we talked with her, we found that Fran was also a very strong, independent person. She had trouble being vulnerable and admitting she needed others, and that tended to keep people at a distance from her. Of course, that added to her feelings of loneliness. Probing deeper, we learned what had helped shape Fran into the strong, somewhat off-putting person she was.

"My father deserted the family when I was seven. I sort of had to be the strong one—to hold the family together, you know." She had done that, and her mother and siblings had been helped by it. But Fran had grown up emotionally before she was ready, and some of her own needs as a child weren't met. Now, years later, she was still carrying that pain as well.

To most people, however, Fran appeared to be as solid as a rock. In addition to what looked like a solid marriage and family, she also had a wonderful ministry as a Bible teacher. She was studying Scripture regularly and instructing others, and they were encouraged and strengthened by her teaching. In spite of that, however, she was struggling with these serious problems in her own life.

We're happy to say that we were able to help Fran, dealing with each concern separately. We called in her husband and did family therapy with both of them. They learned a lot about each other's needs, and they also learned to talk to each other. We helped Fran to see, too, that she had to admit her need for others and let down her guard sometimes. And we guided her in letting God be her loving Father in place of the father she had missed as a child. All this took time, of course, but gradually her depression lifted as she grew in these areas.

Fran's story is a good one to begin this chapter on maintaining wellness because it shows how complex we all are as human beings. It also shows that even when we appear to "have it all together" spiritually, we can still be facing unresolved issues in the present and from as far back as childhood. Fran was clearly growing spiritually in some ways, and physically she was fine, but those were no guarantee of complete or continuing health.

How, then, do we stay healthy once we're making progress or already seem to have a good handle on life? A simple answer would be to say that we keep doing the things that are working, the kinds of things we discussed in the last chapter. But there are other things we can do related to daily habits, and we now explore them in this chapter.

A STRONG MIND AND SPIRIT

A key passage on how to maintain whole health is Colossians 3:1-2: "Since, then, you have been raised with Christ, set your hearts on things above, where Christ is seated at the right hand of God. Set your minds on things above, not on earthly things." Those verses give Christians two commands that can help us to stay mentally and spiritually strong day in and day out.

PRIORITIES THAT HONOR GOD

The first is to "set your hearts on things above." That speaks to us of setting priorities that honor God and are consistent with His will. What things are most important to us? What things are most deserving of our time and effort? If you've never done it, we encourage you to take an hour or two to consider and write down what you think are some God-honoring goals in each area of your life. Take into account the obvious responsibilities He has given you, like time with your family, time with Him, time to care for your body with rest and exercise, and so on. Also consider the talents, gifts, and interests He has given you, and think about how He might want you to use them in ministry if you're not already doing so.

Once you have what you think is a good list, show it to your spouse, talk it through, and get his or her input. If you're not married, do this with a good friend who shares your basic values. Then you can finalize your list.

Keep in mind as you go through this process that the purpose is to help give your life direction in the future; it's not to make you feel guilty about how you've lived in the past. You might decide, however, that some healthy changes are in order, and that's all right. Remember, too, that your priorities can change over time, and that's OK, too. In fact, you should review and revise your list, if necessary, at least once a year.

After you have a list of priorities you feel good about, mentally review what you did in the last week—how you spent your time and energy. You won't remember all the details, but if you go back over each day, you should recall the major blocks of time. Then ask yourself, *In light of what I now want to be my priorities, how did my week compare? Did I spend major time on the most-important goals, or did I spend a lot of time on things that really aren't so important?*

If you're like most people, you'll find you have been spending major time on things of minor importance. So then ask, *How does my life need to shift so that I'm giving my top priorities the attention they deserve?* As you begin to form some conclusions, talk them over with your spouse or close friend as well. We recommend that you compare the way you're using your time to the actual list of priorities once a week so that you don't find yourself straying too far without realizing it.

This kind of evaluation led me (Randy) to make a major career change a few years ago. I had a thriving private medical practice in the Baltimore area, but I was working eighty hours or more a week, and my kids were essentially growing up without a father. When I finally started thinking about what my priorities ought to be, then compared that to how I was currently living, I knew I had to begin putting my family ahead of my work. Eventually I decided to sell the practice, which cut my administrative load and gave me more time at home.

Since that time, my priorities have been refined, as God has shown me the need to place increasingly more priority on family time, personal time with Him, and developing relationships with medical couples. This led to the recent decision to simplify even further my personal and professional lives by accepting a job in a small town in west-central Oregon. Now I work intensely in an emergency room during a straight two-day shift, and then I have five days off every week to focus on my family and ministry to other couples. The time off also lets me pursue hobbies and activities that can aid my own physical, emotional, and spiritual health.

The second command in Colossians 3 is to "set your minds on things above." You'll recall that in the last chapter, we talked about renewing our minds with God's Word. And in chapter 3, we said the mentally healthy person maintains a positive attitude. All these ideas are related, and our corresponding suggestion for staying healthy is to get in the habit of pausing several times each day to ask, *What have I been thinking about recently, especially when my mind has been free to roam where it wanted?*

It's been said, accurately, that our true character is revealed by what we do when no one else is watching. And in the same way, the true state of our thinking is revealed by where our minds turn when they're not preoccupied with something like work or a conversation and can turn wherever they will.

If you find your thought life isn't healthy, look at what you're feeding into it. Perhaps you need to feed it more Scripture, including passages that speak of how highly God values you or that counter whatever unhealthy thoughts you may be dwelling on. If you're preoccupied with a problem, ask, *What is God's perspective on this?*

SCRIPTURE

Memorizing Bible verses can also provide you with true thoughts of who you are, who God is, and how He loves you. The very act of memorizing will cause you to recite aloud and think about the meaning of the Scriptures. You may choose to memorize verses that are especially meaningful to you, or use an organized memory system, such as the Topical Memory System of the Navigators. Daily memorization and meditation on the Scriptures will give your thought life an accurate and healthy perspective of your God and your value to Him.

If a particular, unhealthy thought pattern persists, you should talk it out with someone, perhaps even a professional counselor. Remember, there's nothing wrong with admitting you need help; in fact, it's the healthy thing to do. When Fran realized that her depressive thoughts weren't going away by themselves and that nothing she knew to do helped, she wisely sought help.

Reading Scripture also helps us to determine those priorities that honor God. The apostle Paul encourages us to be wise stewards of our time by understanding "what the will of the Lord is" (see Ephesians 5:15-17, NASB). By knowing His Word we are better able to know His will and priorities on our lives. It is the wise man and woman who make biblical principles a priority of their lives.

GOD IN YOUR DAY

Another good habit that will strengthen our faith is to "look for God" in each day. The idea is to take a few minutes at the end of the day, preferably with your spouse if you're married, and think back over the day's events, looking for places where God's presence and care were evident.

We might remember, for example, that at one point we were tempted to say something cutting, but a small, internal prompting led us to think better. We might recall a near miss in the car when we were spared physically. Perhaps there was a pleasant surprise to be thankful for. Whatever the details on a given day, this mental review will help us to remember God's loving presence in our lives, and that's a very healthy thing to do. Such thoughts are also good for dwelling on as we drift off to sleep.

FORGIVENESS

Another key to mental and spiritual health is to make a habit of forgiving. This is hard, we know, especially if someone has really hurt us. It may take years to get to a point of no longer feeling bitter toward someone who, say, abused us as a child. So we don't want to sound trite or simplistic here. But we know it's God's will that we forgive those who offend us (see Matthew 18: 21-35), so we also know He will give us the strength to do it.

Refusing to forgive can cause serious harm to our health. Harbored bitterness is like a poison that slowly works away inside us. It hurts us *spiritually* because, knowing God wants us to forgive, we find ourselves unable or unwilling to draw close to Him—He would ask us to surrender something we refuse to release. It hurts us *physically* because it leaves us in a constant state of tension, even when we are not aware of it, and that can lead to such ailments as recurring headaches, fatigue, and even ulcers. It also hurts us *mentally,* clouding our judgment and destroying our objectivity, especially (but not exclusively) toward the person who is the object of our acrimony. For all these reasons, it is essential that we forgive. God knew exactly what He was doing when He commanded us to forgive, and as always, His will is what is best for us.

Here again, the wise person who has a problem will admit it and seek help. Part of what Fran needed to do was to forgive the father who had abandoned her years before. Even if she never saw him again, she needed to let go of the bitterness she felt toward him and not let it drag down her heart anymore. She hadn't realized that, but we were able to help her to see it and do it.

Let us emphasize once more, however, that we need to be patient with ourselves. Like a sailor crossing the ocean, we need to be making progress every day, but we shouldn't expect to reach our destination overnight. We like the way John MacArthur, Jr., put it: "It's the direction of our life that counts, not the perfection of our life." God is patient with us when our desire is to obey Him; let's be the same with ourselves.

PRAYER

Meanwhile, let's remember that sound spiritual health includes regular conversation with our God. Just as a healthy family relationship requires that we express our needs and fears to each other, so we need to express our fears and hopes to God. Prayer can occur any time day or night (it's not limited to dinner time) and any place (not just at church). Your prayers will remind you that God wants your time and should be leading your life. Often during prayer we become aware of our motives for wanting something or of an attitude that prevents us from being open to the Lord or other people. Prayer is the welcome breeze of your spiritual health. Breathe deeply.

HEALTHY CHOICES

Finally, a good way to maintain health is to remember that whenever we're in a tough situation, we always have options. Feeling helpless is extremely debilitating; we feel as if we have no control, as if we're at the mercy of someone or something else. But if we realize we have options, we can keep a better frame of mind. Usually you have alternatives; you need only to make the healthy choice.

A doctor came to us one time feeling very depressed. A key reason for his depression was that he felt trapped in a type of medical practice that wore him down day after day; eventually he concluded that he was only "patching people up" and not really healing them. Part of our effort to help him, therefore, was just to show him he had options. He could take more frequent breaks, even if they needed to be briefer. He could ask to be reassigned within his current staff setting. He could always, if nothing else, move to a different type of practice, even if that meant relocating to another town. In his depressed state, he had had a hard time seeing that such options were available.

Sometimes, no easy or safe choice is available. But even then, we choose how we respond to those situations. We are not totally without control.

STAYING PHYSICALLY HEALTHY

TIME FOR EXERCISE

You've probably heard the cliché "Use it or lose it." Well, that certainly applies to physical health. We can exercise ourselves to a given level of fitness, but as soon as we stop, the muscles start to weaken again. Aerobic exercise can develop our heart and lung capacities to a certain point, but as soon as we stop, those capacities will start to drop.

We don't say these things to make exercise sound like a chore. The key to success with it, after all, is to find activities that we enjoy at the same time they're improving or maintaining our health. But fitness does come through exercise. We don't get the benefit without putting in the effort. So exercise needs to become a regular part of our lives, a healthy habit, just like eating well, getting enough rest, keeping our blood pressure under control, and so on. During exercise we can tap into special resources that strengthen our minds and spirits at the same time. Many work out to Christian music tapes. The upbeat, contemporary music helps them maintain their pace, while the lyrics remind them of their Father's love and the promises of help to His followers. You also can enjoy Christian music while jogging, a form of exercise that relieves stress by relaxing muscles, even as it strengthens the heart and the rest of your cardiovascular system. (Fast walking can be just as effective for building and maintaining good physical health.)

Jogging also is an opportunity to meditate on Scripture, either by listening to recorded Scriptures on your Walkman® or repeating verses in your mind. You also can listen to Scripture choruses on your cassette player. Whether walking, jogging, or performing aerobics, you can feed your mind and spirit as well by listening to or reciting Scripture and Christian music.

As we have seen, the physical part of us is closely tied into the spirit and soul, so a failure to maintain physical health will necessarily drag us down in those other areas as well. This means we can't be cavalier about taking care of our bodies except at great risk to the whole person. (For an illustration of how poor physical health can harm the other parts of the whole person, see chapter 10.)

STRESS CONTROL

Another key health issue today is stress and stress control. The pace of modern life, especially here in the Western world, is much faster than it has ever been. The demands on our time, the financial pressures, even the opportunities for entertainment—all are great and getting greater.

Stress can have a number of negative physical effects, but two of the more common are headaches and ulcers. Stress, or tension, headaches tend to come on as the day progresses and the pressures mount. We get frustrated, anxious, and angry, and these emotions cause the brain to send messages to the muscles in the back of the neck and temple areas, telling them to contract and keep contracting beyond their normal limits. That, in turn, causes the pain we call headache. Fortunately, these headaches tend to be of relatively low intensity and can be treated with a bit of aspirin or other over-the-counter pain killer.

Ulcers are a more-serious matter, since they do lasting damage to the stomach, small intestine, and esophagus. Stress can trigger the stomach to produce excess acid, which in turn produces the ulcers. In our clinical experience, more than 60 percent of all ulcers are directly related to stress. And most of the rest of the ulcers are likely indirectly related, since the aspirin-like medications taken to treat headaches and back-aches—many of which are caused by stress—reduce the amount of mucus in the stomach that protects it from its own acid.

A good indicator of the growing frequency of these stress-related problems is that Tagamet has replaced Valium as the most-prescribed medicine in the United States. Tagamet is given for ulcers and other conditions in the stomach, esophagus, and small intestine that cause inflammation and are usually a response to excess acid production.

Therefore, a good way to maintain physical health is to learn how to handle stress better so that we minimize the risk of getting the headaches and, especially, ulcers from which so many others are suffering.

How do we control stress better? Prayer is one of the best ways we know. When we're in a stressful situation, we make a point of asking God for wisdom, strength, and presence of mind to handle things in a way that honors Him. We acknowledge we need His help, and we ask Him for it.

A second way to reduce stress when you're in the middle of an anxiety-producing situation is to take a brief time out for relaxation. Take a few deep breaths. Close your eyes, and imagine you're in a place you find peaceful—perhaps walking along a deserted beach or lying on your back in a flower-filled meadow, looking up at the clouds going by. Let your mind focus on the pleasant sights, sounds, and smells for a minute or so.

Then recall a favorite passage of Scripture that you find comforting or reassuring. Psalm 23 has been a favorite of many people through the years; let your mind dwell on that passage for a minute or two. Finally, thank God for His love and care and His presence with you in the heat of the battle.

Another way to reduce general stress is to look at your priority list again and determine, prayerfully, whether part of your problem is that you're overcommitted or you're devoting too much time and emotional investment to things that aren't your highest priorities anyway. Sometimes we bring a stress overload on ourselves simply by trying to do too much.

One way to reducing general stress is to face up to the things in our lives that cause us pain, confront where confrontation is called for, and make needed changes. The thought of challenging an unreasonable boss, for example, creates a lot of anxiety on several different levels—so much so that our tendency is to keep our mouths shut, continue to try to meet his unfair expectations, and gradually develop an ulcer.

To confront that boss will take courage and a boldness to overcome the fear about what he might say or do. But once we do it (with common sense and Christian love, of course), we'll feel much better about ourselves, we'll relieve the pressure of having all that frustration bottled up inside, and we may even get what we want! Sure, there's risk involved; things may not go the way we'd like. But our health will, without doubt, continue to get worse if we never try to resolve the situation.

Finally, you can confront daily pressure effectively as you put the stressful event into long-term perspective. The apostle Paul emphasizes that we should focus on things of eternal value (2 Corinthians 4:16-18; see our discussion of having God's perspective on pages 111-14 of chapter 8). Three things that have eternal importance are God, God's Word, and our relationships with people. These things can make a difference for eternity; everything else is "small stuff" in comparison. You must ask yourself, "What effect will this have ten years from now, twenty years from now, and in eternity?" Most of the stress-filled issues will lose their intensity when we see them in this eternal perspective. As songwriter Helen Lemmel notes in her great hymn "Turn Your Eyes upon Jesus," "And the things of earth will grow strangely dim in the light of His glory and grace."

PROPER DRUG USE

A final note in this area of physical health has to do with the common misuse of drugs. We are not talking about illegal substance abuse but overdependence on legal drugs, including prescription medications. For example, we have mentioned that the tranquilizer Valium recently has been supplanted as the most-prescribed drug. It remains a common prescription to aid in sleeping. Like most prescribed sedatives, Valium can become addictive through frequent or regular use. Although many people need Valium at least temporarily, many others would be better off and could sleep better if they ate right, got lots of exercise, learned to forgive others, and reduced the stress in their lives.

Perhaps the most frequently consumed drug in the world is caffeine. Present in coffee, tea, and many soft drinks, it's a potent stimulant, and many people use it as such. We all know those folks who can't seem to get started in the morning until they've had the first cup or two of coffee. And just before exam times on college campuses, sales of Mountain Dew take a sharp upturn, as it has the most caffeine of all the nationally distributed soft drinks. (A regional brand, Jolt cola, has even more.)

Used moderately, caffeine probably doesn't do any real harm. Once you get up to four to five cups of coffee per day (or the equivalent), however, the caffeine will create a pharmacologic effect—an addiction. Caffeine tends to constrict the blood vessels, including those in the brain. When a lot of caffeine is ingested regularly, the body adjusts to it; in technical terms, it develops a tolerance. Then the same amount of caffeine will no longer produce the same stimulation. If the caffeine is regularly being taking deliberately for that effect, say by a college student in a series of those late-night cram sessions, more and more will have to be consumed to achieve the desired effect.

If a person cuts back on caffeine usage, withdrawal will occur as with any addictive drug. It's a common situation for a worker to drink a lot of coffee on the job and feel fine, but then, when coffee consumption drops greatly on the weekend, suffer severe headaches. The problem is that without the caffeine constricting those blood vessels in the head, the blood flow suddenly is increased, creating a pressure in the head that in turn produces the headache.

The moral of this story is that we should never forget that caffeine is a powerful drug, and we should treat it as such, making well-thought-out decisions about how and when we use it. Doctors occasionally recommend caffeine for patients, an indication of this drug's physiological effect. Moderate use is always best.

Our theme in this book has been that our three parts are closely connected, so that what happens in one area strongly affects the others as well. To emphasize that principle, we devote the next chapter to further illustrations of how all our parts influence each other, either for good or for ill.

To Your Health

1. Are your goals and priorities what you believe God wants them to be? Why or why not?

2. How does your use of time and energy compare to your goals? What changes, if any, should you consider making?

3. When your mind is free to roam, does it turn to thoughts that are emotionally and spiritually healthy? If not, what can you do today to start reprogramming it?

4. How stressful is your life day to day? List some steps you can take, perhaps including an exercise program, to reduce your stress level.

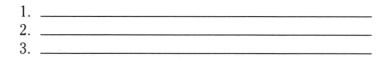

1. _____

2. _____

3. _____

10

PICTURES OF HEALTH AND ILLNESS

One central theme in this book has been that all three parts of each person are intimately connected. Because that's the case, what happens in one part has a direct impact on the other parts as well. Good health in one area helps the other two; however, poor health in one area will drag down the other two with it. To see those two principles in action, let's look at six people on the road to whole health. We have treated several of these patients at our clinics, and their responses demonstrate how each part of our being can influence the others—either for good or for bad.

THE IMPACT OF SPIRITUAL HEALTH

Clara Dawson was a patient of mine (Randy's) several years ago. She was home-bound most of the time, so I had to make old-fashioned house calls to check on her condition and offer what help I could. Yet she was one of the greatest saints I've ever known, and I always left her home thinking I should have paid her for the privilege of our visit.

Clara's physical condition was very poor, her body visited by one ailment after another. She suffered severe rheumatoid arthritis that had deformed her hands and kept her bedridden.

The pain varied in intensity, but it was almost continual; this condition alone makes many people, including Christians, inconsolably bitter. But it was the least of Clara's concerns.

Fifteen years earlier, Clara had developed breast cancer. It had been treated successfully, and she was declared to be in remission. Unknown at the time, however, the cancer had spread to other parts of her body. Now it had reappeared with a vengeance. A mass of cancer was found in her abdomen. By the time it was discovered, it had already penetrated the stomach wall, pushing against that vital organ and causing excruciating pain. She was in such obvious discomfort that it hurt just to watch her.

But in her spirit, Clara Dawson was incredibly strong and healthy. Her unwavering faith in God and His love made time spent with her such a treat that for a while I could almost forget her physical pain—and, for brief moments, Clara could too. Always full of joy, she loved to sing uplifting hymns. She also delighted in writing letters of encouragement and talking to others who would benefit from her testimony of faith and hope.

"This is just a temporary suffering," she reminded her children when they wondered about her pain. "I know that someday I will be with the Lord and have a new body." Her arthritic pain soon meant that she could barely hold a pen, yet she continued to grade Bible correspondence papers for and write personal notes to the children in a local Child Evangelism Fellowship Bible Club. "It was such a blessing to the children when she wrote personal notes that they would write notes back to her and say how much they loved her," says CEF Director Carolyn King.

"Clara, is this too much for you?" Carolyn asked occasionally. Clara's reply never changed: "Well, sometimes it's hard, but it's a blessing to serve the Lord." And with a smile she would add, "When it gets to be too much for me, I'll let you know."

At her funeral, I quoted the Scriptures that capture Clara's outlook on life: "Therefore we do not lose heart. Though outwardly we are wasting away, yet inwardly we are being renewed day by day. For our light and momentary troubles are achieving for us an eternal glory that far outweighs them all. So we fix our eyes not on what is seen, but on what is unseen. For what is seen is temporary, but what is unseen is eternal" (2 Corinthians 4:16-18).

That spiritual conviction, that unshakable hope, lifted Clara emotionally day after day and made her physical struggle relatively insignificant to her. She knew that God has His purposes and that responding to her pain in faith was far more important than getting rid of it. As we've said several times in this book, spiritual health is the most important of all, and Clara Dawson is the best example we know of someone who proved that beyond a doubt. Her strength in that part of her life was far greater than any weakness in the other parts could possibly be.

Unfortunately (but not surprisingly), *poor* spiritual health can have the opposite effect. It can devastate a person physically and emotionally, as well as spiritually.

Mark was a marathon runner, compulsive exerciser, and physical education instructor. To look at him physically, you would call him the picture of health. But that was only a small part of the total picture. When he came in for help, he was feeling physically run down, without energy, and also emotionally depressed. Strong legs, heart, and lungs could not overcome whatever was ailing him.

A battery of physical tests revealed no problem. Lacking an obvious physical disorder, I suspected the cause could be spiritual and decided to present the gospel to Mark. He listened thoughtfully one night and I ended our conversation by saying, "I don't want you to feel pressure. Go home and think about what I said, and in the quietness of your home make a decision."

The next day, Mark became psychotic (detached from reality) and had to be hospitalized, which is not exactly what had been expected! Further examination finally turned up the root of Mark's breakdown. He came from a strict religious background that had instilled in him a highly sensitive conscience. He had a clear, unwavering sense of right and wrong. Yet in recent months, in gross violation of his own standards, he had started and continued in an extramarital affair. Consequently, his spirit was overcome with intense guilt. He had not become a Christian, yet he was confronted with his own sin and thought he had to make atonement. Of course, he could not, but sadly, neither could he accept the forgiveness of his sins that Christ offered. He could not believe that God would forgive him.

Mark was spiritually sick. That spiritual illness led directly to the emotional and physical distress he was experiencing daily. No amount of exercise, healthy food, or positive thinking could rescue him. Only a stoppage of the sinning and reconciliation with his heavenly Father—the restoration of spiritual health—could make him healthy again in any part of his person. To our knowledge, Mark remains psychotic today, a victim of a severe spiritual sickness that has affected every part of his being.

Sarah likewise discovered the hard way how spiritual sickness can also create emotional and physical illness. On her honeymoon—what should have been the happiest time of her life—she started binging on and then purging herself of food (a condition called bulimia). She ate a lot, but she would later excuse herself, go to the bathroom, and intentionally vomit her food. Further, as time went by, Sarah realized she felt no romantic love for her husband and never had.

The root of Sarah's difficulties? Her parents had always been extremely legalistic and controlling, even dictating her choice of a husband. Because they had been that way from her earliest days, she grew to see God in the same manner, as a harsh tyrant. She was actually afraid to get to know Him. And out of this unhealthy fear of God and consequent estrangement from Him had developed her emotional and physical problems as well.

THE IMPACT OF EMOTIONAL HEALTH

A high school English teacher named Barb demonstrated the benefits of emotional health beautifully. Like Clara Dawson, she was found to have cancer that was so far advanced as to make surgery futile. And like Clara, she was a person of strong faith. But besides the support of family and friends, what kept her going for a long time was her love of her students and of teaching.

Barb was determined to continue teaching as long as possible, and her students returned her love. To accommodate her, the school principal first gave her an assigned parking space right by the door she used to enter the school. Then, when she could no longer stand to read aloud to her class (something she and they both enjoyed a great deal), a high stool was provided so she could sit and read. Finally, when she couldn't read for long even sitting down, her students volunteered to do the reading for the rest of their classmates. Fueled by her faith and this kind of love, Barb kept teaching month after month—far longer than her doctor had said would be possible. And she did it without the medication that would have made her too sick in the stomach to teach. Her doctor admitted he didn't know how she kept going.

Eventually, Barb had to reduce her schedule to part time. And ultimately, the cancer took her life. But she had kept going in a productive, love-filled life much longer than anyone could have expected, largely because of her emotional (and spiritual) strength. Physically she was on a slow, sure track to death. But her emotional well-being sustained her far beyond what her doctor expected. And her emotional health sustained her students as well.

On the negative side, we once had a patient named Ron with a serious case of ulcers. He didn't seem to have any bad physical habits that might have caused them, nor did any particular struggles with God appear to be the key. After a time of treating the ulcers and probing his memories for a possible cause, we discovered that his father had molested him as a child. Over the years, Ron's feelings of betrayal, shame, anger toward his father, and even guilt had worked away in his subconscious mind, triggering, among other things, the flow of excess gastric acid that eventually produced his ulcers. He also had a hard time relating to God and believing He loved him and had his best interests at heart. His emotional illness had made him sick all over.

Only by treating his emotional illness could Ron have a complete healing and avoid a recurrence of the ulcer attack. For patients like Ron, we treat the physical problem but also have them enter into counseling. There Ron and others can learn to acknowledge and relinquish the pain and give it up to God. Ron has acknowledged his pain and anger and now is working through the hurt of his childhood abuse and the need to forgive. He is also learning to acknowledge and release the anger and hurt of the childhood abuse. And he is learning the truth about his value in God's eyes. All this will take time.

Another patient was Cindy, an aerobics instructor who seemed to be in great physical condition. In fact, when we sent her to a cardiologist for a stress test, he said she was so fit that she had almost broken his treadmill!

However, Cindy had come in complaining of vomiting and chest and abdominal pains. She was also anorexic and bulimic. All our tests failed to reveal a physical cause of her illness. Clearly, something was deeply troubling this paragon of fitness, who was losing weight and not keeping down her meals.

We began counseling with her, and eventually we learned that her husband was a chronically aloof and insensitive person —so much so that Cindy felt totally rejected, unloved, and unimportant. Those feelings led in turn to a deep depression that manifested itself in her physical illness and in feeling as abandoned by God as she was by her husband.

THE IMPACT OF PHYSICAL HEALTH

To see how good physical health can lift a person emotionally and spiritually, we can turn to a couple of well-known examples. As mentioned in chapter 6, James Dobson, the noted family expert and author, suffered a major heart attack several years ago. A robust, energetic, always-on-the-go kind of person, he had a busy schedule and many responsibilities as president of Focus on the Family. He also had a history of heart disease in his family.

How does that make him a picture of excellent health? Well, Dr. Dobson loves basketball and was in the habit of playing a vigorous game a few times each week. As a result, even though a blockage developed in one of the arteries leading to his heart, causing the heart attack, the heart muscle was strong. Other arteries had grown to supply extra blood to his heart during his robust workouts.

An angiogram, showing the passage of blood through Dobson's coronary arteries, revealed a heart with relatively minor damage considering the extent of the seizure. Of five coronary arteries only one was blocked; meanwhile many smaller blood vessels had formed, "probably from the vigorous exercise I have enjoyed through the years," Dr. Dobson told his friends. The one closed artery "was compensated for by [those] collateral arteries," Dobson explained, concluding: "Basketball it seems, and about a million prayers, saved my life."

Thus, just from a physical standpoint, Dobson was able to survive and recover from the attack in much better shape than would have been the case for most other people.

In addition, his generally strong physical condition helped him deal with the emotional and spiritual sides of recovery in a much more healthy way than many patients we've seen. Because he was strong and knew his recovery was going well, he wasn't so prone to some of the anxiety and questioning of God that's common in such situations. No doubt he had his down moments; that's only natural. But from everything we've read and heard, his good physical health really fortified him in all three areas during his recovery period.

An even better-known example of the pervasive benefits of superb physical shape is former President Ronald Reagan. In 1981, at the age of seventy, he was shot in the chest in an assassination attempt. Fortunately, the bullet just missed doing mortal damage. But Reagan was also helped by the fact that he was in excellent condition, especially for a man of his advanced age. He worked out regularly with weights and kept his own weight under control.

These factors combined to enable him to keep his spirits high and his healthy sense of humor intact even as he was rushed to the hospital and into surgery. While they wheeled him into the operating room, the Republican president said to the doctor who would perform the procedure, "I sure hope you're a Republican!"

On the other hand, poor physical health, especially a chronic illness, can do serious harm to a person's emotional and spiritual condition. Ruth is in her sixties and has been a Christian for many years. For much of her life, she was active in the church and a busy wife and mother. In recent years, however, she has become crippled with arthritis. The illness has affected not only the joints in her hands and legs, but also her lungs, so that the simple breathing most of us take for granted is now a constant struggle for her.

Many of the people that we have described have been able to maintain strong faith and emotional health in spite of such circumstances. Unfortunately, that hasn't been the case with Ruth. The constant pain and unending fight to breathe have worn down every part of her person, but especially her spirit. Chronic pain, whether it be from arthritis, muscular dystrophy, or recurring migraine headaches, can drain an individual to the point that his or her emotions fray and spiritual health flags.

Once a vibrant Christian, Ruth now questions whether God really loves her. She finds no comfort in reading the Bible or in prayer. She knows all the scriptural promises of God's concern and care, but they seem to offer no hope to her. Friends have sought to reassure and encourage her over and over, but their words have no visible effect, and many of them have given up trying.

Emotionally, as you might expect, Ruth is in a constant state of depression. The joy has gone out of her life for the most part, despite her family's best efforts to meet her needs and love her. Her doctors have given her medicines for both her physical and emotional conditions, yet she rarely bothers to take them, so convinced is she that it's no use.

We'd like to be able to report that Ruth is making progress, but she moved away, and we've lost contact. The last we heard, she was still bitter and without hope. Lacking hope, her spirit and soul have also gone slack. As Proverbs 13:12 puts it, "When hope is crushed, the heart is crushed" (GNB*).

Author and pastor Chuck Swindoll summarizes well our state when we lose hope. "Take from a man his wealth, and you hinder him; take from him his purpose, and you slow him down. But take from a man his hope and you stop him. He can go without wealth and even without purpose for a little while. But he will not go on without hope."[1]

A TIME FOR ACTION

As the stories in this chapter demonstrate, all three parts that make up our person are vital. We can't neglect any one of them without suffering the consequences in the other two as well. Strength in one part, especially the spirit, can help to overcome weakness in one or more of the others. Clara Dawson is a prime example of that. But the converse is also true: Poor health in one part can do additional, dramatic damage in the others. Mark, Sarah, Ron, Cindy, and Ruth are all proof of this fact.

Our encouragement to you, therefore, is to go back to the self-test in chapter 3 and see what areas of your health need work. If you haven't already completed "Your Health Profile," do so now. And then formulate a realistic plan that you will be able to stick with over time and that will begin to strengthen your health in every area, starting with the weakest.

No one else can do it for you, and there's no better time than now.

*Good News Bible

To Your Health

1. What might account for the different reactions of Clara Dawson and Ruth to their chronic illnesses?

2. If you could give one piece of practical counsel to Sarah (who had the overcontroling parents and fear of God), what would it be? Why?

3. Maybe you know someone whose poor physical health is causing him or her to despair of God's care. Citing Scripture or inviting the person to church will not, in itself, change a spiritual condition. But attending to the person's physical needs may free the person to consider his emotional and spiritual needs. List three things you can do to offer the person physical comfort. (Remember, even listening to the person talk and cooking meals qualify as physical help.)

    1. _____
    2. _____
    3. _____

4. If you have frequent pain or emotional depression, you too are vulnerable to a more general decline of health. Based on the cautions of this chapter and the recommendations of chapter 9, list a plan of action to deal with the ailment.

    1. _____
    2. _____
    3. _____

Further medical treatment and/or professional counseling may be needed. If you are unable to list a plan or feel incapable of action, we strongly urge you to seek professional help. The next chapter will give guidelines for finding such help.

11

GETTING HELP

Like a lot of people, Sam was under a great deal of stress. He had a demanding job in a highly technical field, purchasing precision parts for a manufacturer of state-of-the-art medical testing equipment. And he was just coming back to that line of work after several years of pursuing another venture. In that other career, he had experienced what he considered to be serious failure; his consulting business had gone bankrupt. As a result of all this, he was insecure, feeling inadequate, and worried about his future. Obviously, Sam was going through some rough times. But so do a lot of people, and most of them never go looking for professional help to deal with their struggles. Sam did, and we think he was wise to do so.

What accounts for the difference? Couldn't a friend have helped him out? What are the limits to such help? Why was it, in his case, good for him to come to a doctor? And when Sam decided to look for help, how important was it that the helper be a fellow Christian?

WHAT A FRIEND CAN DO

Suppose you were a friend of Sam's and you noticed that he seemed extremely anxious. Or maybe you recognized that

Sam was using one of the common defense mechanisms described in chapter 5, perhaps denial. As a caring friend, what could you do to help?

First, you must decide whether you are willing to pay the price to be a real help. That price will be paid in time, in an investment of emotional energy, and perhaps in convenience if he needs to talk at a time when you had other plans. If Sam is using a defense mechanism, he may at first resent your efforts to help him see the truth, and then you would have some pain of rejection to deal with as well.

We don't mean to paint a bleak picture of what it costs to help a friend, for there is also a great sense of joy and satisfaction that comes with it. We think, too, that the inconvenience, even discomfort, of helping others is a part of what the apostle Paul had in mind when he instructed us to "carry each other's burdens" (Galatians 6:2). Just a few verses later he added, "Let us not become weary in doing good, for at the proper time we will reap a harvest if we do not give up. Therefore, as we have opportunity, let us do good to all people, especially to those who belong to the family of believers" (vv. 9-10).

In a similar vein, Jesus said, "A new commandment I give you: Love one another. As I have loved you, so you must love one another. All men will know that you are my disciples if you love one another" (John 13:34-35).

We believe that if Christians took those passages seriously and reached out to one another with loving compassion, many of the struggles that end up being handled in the offices of counselors, psychologists, and medical doctors could be worked out within the church. That's the biblical model, and that's what we'd love to see. But we do want you to understand that there are costs involved.

The second step is to evaluate the nature of your friendship. Is the trust between you deep enough so that the hurting person would feel free to discuss his problems with you? In other words, have you earned the right to get involved in his life? If not, the third step has to be the development of such a trust. Otherwise, the person will never open up to you.

The type of relationship we're talking about is one in which Sam knows that you will love him no matter what he tells you or what he might be doing. He has to know that whatever he reveals, you will accept him and be loyal rather than judge him. Anyone you may help needs to know that you will provide a safe environment in which he can say anything and not be rejected or fear a betrayal of confidence.

That type of trust grows gradually, as you do things together and as he first shares smaller confidences and finds you to be accepting. This takes some time. So if such a relationship doesn't already exist between you and Sam when you see he needs help and you want to respond, you'll have to take the time and effort to earn his trust.

I (Randy) remember receiving such love for the first time. As a child and teen, having been abandoned by my father when I was quite young, I was a real rabble rouser. I was looking for attention, trying to be popular, and going about it in a lot of wrong ways. Most adults responded to me as you would expect. But the parents of one girl I dated in high school were different.

They were Christians (I wasn't at the time), and their relationship with Jesus truly shaped the way they lived. They gave me a degree of love and acceptance I had never known before—not from my father, and not even from my mother. I really tested their love, too. A couple of times, they found beer cans in their car from my late-night outings. Once they found a men's magazine in their daughter's drawer that I had given her.

If I had been her father, I think I would have booted me out many times and said, "Don't ever come back again!" But they took me on picnics, family outings, and vacations, and they encouraged me to go to church. They never shoved the Bible down my throat, but they answered my questions about it, and they just loved me.

Their acceptance and their example were what opened my heart to hearing the gospel and responding. I'm a Christian today in large part because of the way they chose to love me in spite of my shortcomings. And that's the kind of influence you can have on hurting hearts as well. People will respond and welcome your help when they know that your care and love are genuine.

When the trust has been established, the next step is to be a good listener. Many times, such as when a person is grieving the loss of a loved one or has been laid off from a job, the individual just needs to talk things out, to express the pain and know that someone hears and cares. You may not feel you're "doing" a lot to help in such a case, but just being there and being attentive is the best thing you can do at that time. Counselors will tell you that many clients are paying them mostly just to be the sympathetic listeners they can't find anywhere else.

Sometimes, though—such as when the person is avoiding his pain with a defense mechanism—you'll need to probe gently for the cause. "Who has hurt you?" "What's got you so anxious?"

Consider Sam, now returning to work after being in a different business that failed. If you were Sam's friend, and he seemed to be denying his pain, you might need to identify with it and "give him permission" to be anxious. You could say something like, "Sam, you seem a little worried about how your new job is going. I know it's tough starting a new job, especially when you've been doing a different kind of work for a while. I'd be nervous, too."

Then he's likely to feel a little safer. It may take a while, though, and he may say, "Yeah, I've been worried some. Is it showing?" Once he makes that admission, bit by bit the person usually opens up, and you can begin to talk about a healthy way of handling the pain.

In Sam's case, he would be helped by learning to focus his mind on God's love and promises to provide (such as the promises in Matthew 6:25-34). Some of the techniques for handling stress that we mentioned in the preceding chapter could also help. Maybe he needs to work through some bitterness and offer forgiveness toward others—even God—for the failure he experienced in his previous line of work. Primarily, Sam would be helped by growing in his trust in God's faithfulness and care.

Let us emphasize again that this kind of care-giving on your part (and growth on Sam's part) will take time. Don't expect one Bible study to "do the trick." Don't expect him to move from anxiety to a-pillar-of-faith kind of trust in God in a day or a week. Be patient with the process, and be patient with Sam.

WHEN PROFESSIONAL HELP IS NEEDED

The kind of friend-to-friend care we have described above will be all the help most people need. But there are times when it's not enough. Those times fall into two general categories.

First, professional help is called for if the person's problem is affecting him physically. When such problems appear, lay care usually is not enough. In Sam's case, his extreme anxiety was producing several physical effects. One was insomnia. By the time he came for help, he had gone four months without being able to sleep more than two or three hours per night. That's not enough sleep for anyone, and an anxious person needs even more sleep than usual. You can imagine how his health, his family life, and his work performance were all suffering.

Sam had other physical complications as well, including occasional abdominal pain and heart palpitations. All these were clear indications, especially since they were happening at the same time and were ongoing, that he needed to see a doctor.

The second case in which professional help is called for is when you, as the helping friend, start to feel uncomfortable about how the person is doing mentally or emotionally. If you were trying to help Sam, for instance (assuming for the moment that he didn't have the obvious physical need for a doctor), and his self-image seemed fragile, or he seemed to be getting more insecure instead of improving, or he seemed to be wavering and unstable—in that case you would probably begin to feel you were in over your head. And you would almost certainly be right.

Then you would want to encourage Sam to seek the help of a professional counselor. But again, don't come across as judgmental or alarmist. Simply say, "You know, Sam, I think you need some further help to work things out, help that I'm just not trained to provide. A good counselor could probably do a lot more for you." As you get involved in caring for others, it's good to remember that you have that option. No one is asking you to try to do more than you are able. You can do a lot of good, but there is a time when trained professional help is really needed. Don't be afraid to admit that and refer a friend. Your pastor can recommend good counselors in your area.

DOES THE PROFESSIONAL NEED TO BE A CHRISTIAN?

The importance of a professional helper's faith depends on the kind of help that's needed. If the problem is strictly physical—asthma, a heart problem, or whatever—the doctor's faith isn't a crucial issue. Your main concern then is to find the most competent doctor you can. With medical education what it is today, most physicians are well trained and competent. And if they've been board certified in their specialty, they're highly likely to be good doctors.

One exception to the rule of looking only for great competence in physicians might come when you're choosing an obstetrician/gynecologist. Then, as a matter of principle, you may want to make a point of going to someone who does not perform abortions, who is dedicated to preserving life and not destroying it. Again, any board-certified doctor is likely to be highly competent, so you're not losing much in that regard by standing on principle.

The answer is entirely different, however, if the helper needed is a psychologist or psychiatrist. We would much rather go to a Christian psychiatrist, if we needed such assistance, than to a non-Christian who was a more-capable psychopharmacologist (that is, a doctor treating mental disorders with appropriate medications).

The reason, of course, is that these specialists are dealing with a patient's mind, thoughts, emotions, and values. Non-Christians will be using humanistic presuppositions that likely won't include God or be based on a biblical value system. They may be ethical and generally upright practitioners, but that's not the same as seeing people from God's perspective and drawing on His resources as part of the healing process.

Many secular schools of psychiatry, for example, still provide a heavily Freudian training perspective. And while Freud had some good insights into the human mind and personality, he described himself as a "godless Jew." Not surprisingly, therefore, his primary presuppositions were wrong. Consequently, his views of how to treat mental problems were also seriously flawed. His followers also are working with severely flawed approaches to restoring mental and emotional health.

All this means that when our problems are mental, emotional, or certainly spiritual in nature, the faith of the helper is a vital issue. He or she simply must share our Christian perspective. Hopefully we can find someone who is both a Christian *and* competent. And here again, pastors should be able to provide good referrals.

We hope this discussion has encouraged you to reach out to those around you who are hurting and could be aided tremendously by a caring friend. You can do far more good than you probably realize. But you also need wisdom about when help is needed beyond what you can give.

If you are yourself hurting, we hope this chapter has bolstered your courage to look for a friend who can help meet your needs. And if you realize you need professional help, don't hesitate to seek it out. We *all* need help at times; you're not alone in that. Ask for God's assistance, and He will guide you to a good helper.

As we near the end of this book, we've seen a picture of whole-person health; we've examined what often goes wrong in our pursuit of health; and we've considered how to move from our present level of health toward a greater degree of wellness. In the next chapter, we will go back and revisit Suzy Morgan in the midst of her trials and tribulations. What if Suzy had read this same book, analyzed her life in light of it, and begun to apply its principles? How might she handle her struggles of everyday life—the same kinds of hassles we all face—differently?

In the final chapter, let's watch as Suzy faces her day's tensions using these biblical principles for being a whole person.

To Your Health

1. Think of a friend, relative, or acquaintance who could use some help right now. Do you have a level of trust established such that you could help? If not, how could you develop such a relationship?

2. Realistically, are you willing and able to give the time and energy needed to help? If not, why not?

3. How good a listener do you think you are? For a second opinion, ask the person closest to you—your spouse, other family member, or a friend—for his or her assessment of your listening skills.

4. List some feelings or behaviors a friend might have that would make you uncomfortable and indicate that he or she might need professional help.

    1. _____

    2. _____

    3. _____

12

A Day in a Healthy Life

In chapters 1 and 2 we looked at one eventful day in the life of Suzy Morgan. As we saw, when she faced a series of conflicts that busy Monday morning, she wasn't exactly the picture of health in any area. But let's assume now that before that day arrived, Suzy had heard the same ideas you've read in this book, and she took them to heart. She had been growing ever since. So let's see how she would handle that same kind of difficult day differently as a result. Compare her thoughts and feelings now to those in chapters 1 and 2.

ANOTHER MONDAY

It was just another Monday morning in the Morgan household. Nothing unusual was happening—just Suzy and Roger and the twins, Billy and Brad, trying to get ready for the day. The weekend had been good, but this day got off to a rough start, especially for Suzy.

Her morning started at 4:30 A.M., when the neighbor's dog started barking loudly yet again. Spot was making another early-morning run. Once she was awakened, Suzy, a light sleeper but a healthy, positive person, knew she wouldn't be able to get back to sleep. *Silly dog. I should have known—.* She laughed at herself, knowing her day had now unofficially begun. So she decided to make the most of her time. She slipped into her sweatsuit, did some stretching exercises, and then went into the kitchen.

After brewing a pot of decaffeinated coffee, Suzy grabbed her Bible and study guide and sat down with half a bagel and a banana. *Might as well work on my study for Wednesday night*, she figured. She stayed at that for about an hour, at the end of which she prayed. Among other things, she asked God to give her the strength to get through the day on less-than-usual sleep.

Next she prepared a hot breakfast for the family and put it in the oven to stay warm before anyone else got up. *Hey, maybe I should do this more often!* she thought. *Saves a lot of rushing around when everybody else is trying to get ready.*

As soon as she got the twins up, Suzy had to start playing referee. Billy, who was hitting Brad in the behind with his pillow, stopped instantly when Suzy told him, "You know, Grandma told me your father acted just like that when he was your age."

As Suzy walked back into the bedroom after serving the kids' breakfast, Roger said, "Honey, a button just came off this shirt. You know it's my favorite, and I've got a big meeting today. Can you sew it back on real quick? I know I should learn how to do this myself, especially with you working now, but—"

Suzy put her hands on her hips and stared at him.

Roger smiled and said, "Are you trying to tell me something? You know, you look just like your mother when you do that, and she's the second-most-beautiful woman I've ever seen."

Suzy groaned, but then she couldn't help laughing as she thought about how she'd used a similar line on Billy. "We're not above cheap manipulation, are we?" she joked. "Well, I can be bought with flattery, but *you've* got to make sure the twins put their dishes in the sink and brush their teeth."

"Fair enough," he conceded, heading for the kitchen. Suzy chuckled as she heard him trying to break up a toothpaste war a few minutes later.

Not long after, Suzy was herding the kids into the car when she noticed a run in one leg of her pantyhose. *No time to look for another pair now,* she realized. *I guess I know how I'll be spending part of my lunch hour.*

When Suzy pulled into Billy and Brad's preschool parking lot, a familiar twinge of regret passed through her mind. "Lord," she prayed, "You know I wouldn't be leaving them here if I had a choice. But until we pay off the debt from Roger's business bankruptcy, I have to do this. Watch over them, I pray. Thank You for leading us to this place where the staff can show them Your love and care for them almost as much as Roger and I do. And thank You for helping me negotiate a flexible schedule with my boss so I can take care of the kids' special needs when they come up."

Suzy arrived at work right on time. As she passed the office of Mr. Taylor, her boss, she noticed him glancing out at her and then at his desk clock.

When Suzy got to her desk, Gwen, her best friend in the office, was waiting for her. "Mr. Taylor is making note of late-comers again, trying to see who he can give a hard time to," Gwen said. "He's such a stickler for the rules. How did you say you managed to talk him into giving us flextime?"

Suzy smile and acknowledged Gwen. Then she prayed silently, "Thank You again for that. Help me to explain Your love to Gwen once more, and draw her to Yourself." To Gwen she said, "I've got to run to the drugstore at lunch. Why don't you come with me? We'll grab something to eat on the way back, and I'll tell you all about it."

At the end of her workday, Suzy was driving home (Roger was picking up the twins this one time) when her car stalled just as she got to the railroad crossing. It coasted to a stop right on top of the tracks. *What's going on?* she wondered. Then she glanced at the fuel gauge and saw she was out of gas.

Oh, no! she thought. *Roger used this car last night, and he was supposed to put gas in the tank! Am I ever going to have something to say to him when I get home!*

Suzy put the gearshift in park and tried to start it again, but nothing happened. *Well,* she figured, *at least there's no train coming. Maybe if I go over to that gas station on the corner—.*

Just then she heard the clang, clang of the warning bells and saw the crossing gates starting to come down. Spinning her head to the left, she could hear the rumble of an approaching train. "Oh, Lord," she prayed quickly, "what do I do now?"

All of a sudden her heart was racing, and sweat broke out on her forehead. She decided to try starting the car again, but it was no use. Finally, as she saw the train coming around a bend toward her, she yanked on the door handle, flung the door open, leaped out of the car, and ran until she was safely beyond the gate.

As she stood and watched the approaching train, she prayed, "Lord, that car is almost new! We've only made three payments on it. The insurance won't cover the full replacement cost! Make that train stop in time, please!"

A few seconds later, its brakes screaming, the train plowed into Suzy's new Chevy. Suzy heard the impact but didn't see it through her squeezed-shut, hand-covered eyes. When she looked again, her demolished car was lying beside the track fifty yards from where she had left it.

Suzy started to cry, a mixture of sadness and relief. After looking at it for a minute, the car oddly reminded her of a modern sculpture she had seen and liked recently. She had to smile at the thought.

Taking a deep breath, Suzy prayed, "Well, Lord, I don't know why You let that happen. But You helped us get the car, and I trust You to help us work things out again. I guess I should thank You that I was able to get out safely—and thank You that the kids weren't with me!"

Smiling again, Suzy thought, *I guess this will teach Roger to put gas in the car when he's supposed to! I can't wait to hear him explain this one to his brother!*

HEALTHY PEOPLE KEEP SMILING

Like Suzy, we're all going to have rough days, and we're all going to have pain. For reasons we don't always understand, God allows trials to come into our lives. But we know enough about Him, through His Word and human experience, that we can continue to trust Him and reach out to Him even then.

Last year while we (the Reeses) were away on vacation, someone entered our Richardson, Texas, home and set a fire. We still don't know who the vandal was, but the arsonist took a few items and the fire ruined much of our home; property damage alone totaled more than $400,000. Already devastated by this loss, my wife, Bonnie, and I were then subjected to a deep, sometimes hostile interrogation by our insurance company, who implied we might have started the fire ourselves for financial gain. An investigator scrutinized our financial records and questioned friends and businesses about our dealings.

The whole process wore us emotionally, physically, and financially. We could no longer occupy our home. Our three daughters were uprooted from their neighborhood and friends. Furthermore, the home invasion attacked Bonnie's and my sense of security. And if the company refused to cover our losses, we would have no home and probably have to file for bankruptcy. After several delays and the possibilty of nonpayment by the insurance company, the insurers finally agreed to repay most of the losses.

Yet through all this, the Reeses found comfort that sustains—from friends and a God who cares greatly. Our greatest comfort came from God's Word. The morning of the fire, I read "Fear not, for you will not be put to shame; neither feel humiliated; for you will not be disgraced . . . If anyone fiercely assails you, it will not be from Me" (Isaiah 54: 4, 15; NASB). Later that evening, when I found out about the fire, that verse gave me assurance that God was there, protecting us. Over the weeks several portions of Isaiah helped us. I often reviewed Isaiah 43:2: "When you pass through the waters I will be with you; and through the rivers, they will not overflow you. When you walk through the fire, you will not be scorched." I knew He was there and would walk us through it, holding our hands.

For three weeks we were crammed in a motel as the builders determined the extent of the damage and prepared cost estimates for repairing the house. We had only three changes of clothes (left from our vacation), and the children had no room to do their homework once school resumed. They began to complain, with good reason, as they literally bumped into one another in the narrow spaces. Even then, God's Word gave comfort, as Bonnie and I read Isaiah 49:20: "The children born during your bereavement will yet say in your hearing, 'This place is too small for us; give us more space to live in.' " That perfect description of our situation made us smile (even though the following six months we stayed in a temporary rental house as the builders repaired our home).

And you too can keep smiling through the pain. We all can use the resources God provides, from our own healthy habits and the help of Christian friends and professionals, to His Word, to face our problems, deal with them directly and wisely, and move on.

We can enjoy life to the fullest, as we're developing true whole-person health day by day.

TO YOUR HEALTH

1. The main events of Suzy's day were not noticeably different in this chapter compared to the events in chapters 1 and 2. But her responses were. List the different actions Suzy took in response to her problems. (Review chapters 1 and 2, if necessary.)

    1. _____
    2. _____
    3. _____
    4. _____

2. What was the biggest difference between the two days?

3. What would you say is the healthiest thing about Suzy?

4. If the healthy Suzy were your friend, what advice do you think she would offer you today? Summarize Suzy's advice in the blank below.

_____

_____

_____

Appendix A

COMMONLY PRESCRIBED
MEDICATIONS

Psychotropic medications, which act on the brain, can be a vital part of the healing process when properly administered by a physician. They don't "alter your mind" in any negative sense but rather help to restore the normal functioning of the brain, whose chemical balances are changed by prolonged anxiety, depression, and other illnesses.

Some of the commonly prescribed medications are listed on the following pages with the type of illness for which they're given (clinical use) and the potential adverse mental and emotional reactions that may occur. The brand name is listed first. (Some drugs are available under more than one brand name.) In some cases, generic names or active ingredients (aspirin and codeine, for example) are shown. Then, because most drugs can have adverse side effects if abused, taken in the wrong dosage, or just depending on individual physiology, some of the possible psychiatric reactions are given. These are not meant to scare you but to emphasize that all drugs need to be used carefully, and that these prescription drugs need to be taken only under close medical supervision.

INDICATIONS AND ADVERSE REACTIONS OF SOME COMMONLY USED MEDICATIONS

MEDICATION	CLINICAL USE	ADVERSE MENTAL AND EMOTIONAL REACTIONS								
		Depression	Anxiety	Insomnia	Night	Mania	Psychosis/Halluc.	Paranoia	Conf.	Agit.
Accutane	Acne	●								
Actifed	Nasal Allergies							●		
Afrin	Nasal Congestion		●	●			●			
Amitriptyline	Depression					●	●	●		
Amphetamines	Hyperactivity; Depression	●	●			●	●	●		●
Antihistamines	Allergic Conditions		●				●			
Aspirin	Inflammation; Pain						●	●	●	●
Atarax	Anxiety; Allergies		●				●			
Barbiturates	Anxiety	●					●			
Caffeine	Stimulant: Pain; Migraine		●				●		●	
Centrax	Anxiety	●		●	●		●	●		●

LEGEND: Night = Nightmares   Haluc. = Hallucinations   Conf. = Confusion   Agit. = Agitation

ADVERSE MENTAL AND EMOTIONAL REACTIONS

MEDICATION	CLINICAL USE	Depression	Anxiety	Insomnia	Night	Mania	Psychosis/Halluc.	Paranoia	Conf.	Agit.
Codeine	Pain Relief	●	●		●		●	●		●
Cortisone	Allergic/Inflammatory Conditions	●				●	●	●	●	
Dalmane	Insomnia	●		●	●		●	●		●
Darvon	Pain Relief	●	●		●		●	●		●
Desyrel	Depression					●	●	●		
Dexatrim	Obesity	●	●			●	●	●		●
Dilantin	Seizures	●				●	●		●	●
Doral	Insomnia	●		●	●	●	●	●		●
Elavil	Depression			●		●	●	●		
Halcion	Insomnia	●		●	●		●	●		●
Inderal	Hypertension; Heart Arrhythmias; Migraine	●			●	●	●	●	●	
Klonopin	Anxiety; Compulsiveness	●		●	●		●	●		●

ADVERSE MENTAL AND EMOTIONAL REACTIONS

MEDICATION	CLINICAL USE	Depression	Anxiety	Insomnia	Night	Mania	Psychosis/Halluc.	Paranoia	Conf.	Agit.
Librium	Anxiety	●		●	●		●	●		●
Lithium	Manic-Depressive/ Bipolar Disorder						●		●	
Ludiomil	Depression						●			
Motrin	Inflammation; Pain	●	●				●	●	●	●
Nardil	Depression; Panic		●			●		●		●
NeoSynephrine	Nasal Congestion	●					●	●		
Norpramin	Depression					●	●	●		
Pamelor	Depression					●	●	●		
Penicillin	Infections	●	●				●		●	●
Pepcid	Ulcers; Acid Indigestion	●				●	●	●	●	
Phenergan	Nausea						●			
Phenobarbital	Seizures	●				●	●		●	●
Prednisone	Allergic/Inflammatory Conditions	●				●	●	●	●	

ADVERSE MENTAL AND EMOTIONAL REACTIONS

MEDICATION	CLINICAL USE	Depression	Anxiety	Insomnia	Night	Mania	Psychosis/Halluc.	Paranoia	Conf.	Agit.
Prozac	Depression					●				
Ritalin	Hyperactivity; Depression; Narcolepsy		●					●		
Sinequan	Depression					●	●	●		
Tagamet	Ulcers; Acid Indigestion	●				●	●	●	●	
Tenormin	Hypertension	●			●	●	●	●	●	
Thyroid	Hypothyroidism	●	●			●	●	●		
Tofranil	Depression					●	●	●		
Transderm Scopolamine	Motion Sickness		●				●	●		●
Valium	Anxiety	●		●	●		●	●	●	●
Ventolin	Asthma; Emphysema						●	●		
Vistaril	Anxiety; Allergies		●				●			
Vivactil	Depression					●	●	●		
Zantac	Ulcers; Acid Indigestion	●				●	●	●	●	

Modified and adapted from "Drugs That Cause Psychiatric Symptoms," *The Medical Letter on Drugs and Therapeutics* 31 (December 29, 1989): 113-16. Used by permission. The Medical Letter, 56 Harrison St., New Rochelle, New York 10801.

Appendix B

MEDICAL REFERENCES: A BIBLIOGRAPHY

American Medical Association. *Encyclopedia of Medicine.* New York: Random House, 1989. Also Boston: Houghton, Mifflin, 1991.

Herbert, Victor, and Stephen Barret. *Vitamins and Health Foods: The Great American Hustle.* Philadelphia: George F. Stickley, 1985

Hunt, Dave, and T. A. McMahon. *America: The Sorcerer's New Apprentice.* Eugene, Oreg.: Harvest, 1988.

McIlhaney, Joe, with Susan Nethery. *Twelve Hundred Fifty Health-Care Questions Women Ask.* Grand Rapids: Baker, 1985.

Martin, Walter. *The New Age Cult.* Minneapolis: Bethany, 1989.

NOTES

CHAPTER 2: What We're Made Of

1. W. E. Vine, *Vine's Expository Dictionary of New Testament Words* (McLean, Va.: MacDonald, n.d.), p. 1,077.

2. Gary Smalley and John Trent, *The Two Sides of Love* (Pomona, Calif.: Focus on the Family, 1990), p. 166.

CHAPTER 3: The Picture of Health

1. Herman Tyroler, "Overview of Clinical Trials of Cholesterol-Lowering in Relationship to Epidemiologic Studies," *American Journal of Medicine* 87 (supplement 4A; October 16, 1989): n.p.

2. Ibid. See also "Lipid Research Clinics Coronary Primary Prevention Results, *Journal of American Medical Association* 251 (1984): 351-73; and M. H. Frick, O. Elo, K. Haapa, et al. "Helsinki Health Study," *New England Journal of Medicine* 317 (1987): 1, 237-45.

CHAPTER 4: Where Our Trouble Begins

1. M. Scott Peck, *The Road Less Traveled* (New York:Simon & Schuster, 1978), p. 15.

2. Stephen Brown, *If God Is in Charge* (Nashville: Nelson, 1983), p. 39.

3. Shannon Brownlee and Joanne Silberner, "The Age of Genes," *U.S. News & World Report*, November 4, 1991, p. 64.

4. Sharon Begley, "Mapping the Brain," *Newsweek*, April 20, 1992, p. 66.

5. Norm Wright, *Communication: Key to Your Marriage* (Glendale, Calif.: Regal, 1974), pp. 62-63.

6. Philip Yancey, *Disappointment with God* (Grand Rapids: Zondervan, 1988), p. 23.

7. Bill Hybels, *Honest to God?* (Grand Rapids: Zondervan, 1990), p. 102.

CHAPTER 6: False Hopes for Physical Health

1. Claudia Wallis, "Why New Age Medicine is Catching On," *Time*, November 4, 1991, p.73.

2. Ibid.

3. Ibid., pp. 68-76; Steven Findlay, Doug Podolsky, and Joanne Silberner, "Wonder Cures from the Fringe," and Doug Podolsky, "Big Claims, No Proof," *U.S. News & World Report*, September 23, 1991, pp. 68-77. Much of the information in this section comes from the *Time* ("Why New Age Medicine Is Catching On") and *U.S. News & World Report* ("Big Claims, No Proof") articles.

4. Findlay et al., "Wonder Cures from the Fringe," p. 71.

5. Ibid., p. 69.

CHAPTER 7: An Old New Age Deceit

1. Karen Hoyt, *The New Age Rage* (Old Tappan, N.J.: Revell, 1987), pp. 177-78.

2. Ibid., p. 11.

3. Ibid., p. 18.

4. Ibid., p. 32.

CHAPTER 8: Moving from Sickness to Health

1. M. Scott Peck, *The Road Less Traveled* (New York: Simon & Schuster, 1978), p. 17.

2. Archibald Hart, *Depression: Coping and Caring* (Arcadia, Calif.: Cope, 1981), p. 57.

3. "American Cancer Guidelines on Diet, Nutrition and Cancer," *Ca—A Cancer Journal for Clinicians* 41 (November/December 1991): 336.

4. L. Garfinkel "Overweight and Cancer," *Annals of Internal Medicine* 103 (1985): 1034-39; as quoted in "American Cancer Guidelines on Diet, Nutrition and Cancer," *Ca—A Cancer Journal for Clinicians* 41 (November/December 1991): 335. The Garfinkel study also found that obese women had an 87 percent higher mortality rate for all causes of death than nonobese women. The same mortality rate was found for obese men compared with nonobese men.

CHAPTER 10: Pictures of Health and Illness

1. Charles Swindoll, *Dropping Your Guard* (Waco, Texas: Word, 1986), p. 192.